# CONTINENTS IN CLOSE-UP

# AFRICA

## MALCOLM PORTER and KEITH LYE

### CHERRYTREE BOOKS

A Cherrytree Book

Designed and produced by
AS Publishing
Text by Keith Lye
Illustrated by Malcolm Porter and Raymond Turvey

First published 1999
by Cherrytree Press Limited
a subsidiary of
The Chivers Company Limited
Windsor Bridge Road
Bath BA2 3AX

Copyright © Malcolm Porter and AS Publishing

British Library Cataloguing in Publication data

Porter, Malcolm
   Africa. - (Continents in close-up)
   1.Children's atlases 2.Africa - Maps for children
   I.Title II.Lye, Keith
   912.6

ISBN 0 7540 9033 7

Printed in Italy by L. E. G. O.

# CONTINENTS IN CLOSE-UP

# AFRICA

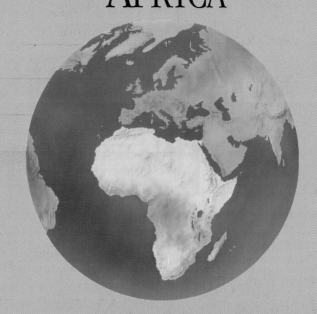

This illustrated atlas combines maps, pictures, flags, globes,
information panels, diagrams and charts to give an overview
of the whole continent and a closer look at each of its countries.

## COUNTRY CLOSE-UPS

Each double-page spread has these
features:

**Introduction** The author introduces the
most important facts about the country
or region.

**Globes** A globe on which you can see the
country's position in the continent and the
world.

**Flags** Every country's flag is shown.

**Information panels** Every country has an
information panel which gives its area,
population and capital, and where
possible its currency, religions, languages,
main towns and government.

**Pictures** Important features of each
country are illustrated and captioned to
give a flavour of the country. You can
find out about physical features, famous
people, ordinary people, animals, plants,
places, products and much more.

**Maps** Every country is shown on a
clear, accurate map. To get the most out
of the maps it helps to know the symbols
which are shown in the key on the
opposite page.

**Land** You can see by the colouring on
the map where the land is forested,
frozen or desert.

**Height** Relief hill shading shows where
the mountain ranges are. Individual
mountains are marked by a triangle.

**Direction** All of the maps are drawn
with north at the top of the page.

**Scale** All of the maps are drawn to scale
so that you can find the distance
betweeen places in miles or kilometres.

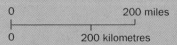

| 0 | | 200 miles |
|---|---|---|
| 0 | | 200 kilometres |

# KEY TO MAPS

| | |
|---|---|
| **KENYA** | Country name |
| ~~~ | Country border |
| ■ | More than 1 million people* |
| • | More than 500,000 people |
| • | Less than 500,000 people |
| □ | Country capital |
| ATLAS MTS | Mountain range |
| ▲ Kilimanjaro 5895m | Mountain with its height |

*Many large cities, such as Johannesburg, have metropolitan populations that are greater than the city figures. Such cities have larger dot sizes to emphasize their importance.*

| | |
|---|---|
| Nile | River |
| ┬┬┬ | Canal |
| ⬭ | Lake |
| ┼ | Dam |
| ⬭ | Island |

| | |
|---|---|
| | Forest |
| | Crops |
| | Dry grassland |
| | Desert |
| | Tundra |
| | Polar |

## CONTINENT CLOSE-UPS

**People and Beliefs** Map of population densities; chart of percentage of population per country; chart of areas of countries; map of religions; pie-chart of main religious groups.

**Climate and Vegetation** Map of vegetation from forests to deserts; maps of winter and summer temperatures; map of annual rainfall.

**Ecology and Environment** Map of environmental damage to land and sea; map of natural hazards and diseases; panel of endangered animals and plants.

**Economy** Map of agricultural and industrial products; pie-chart of gross national product for individual countries; panel on per capita gross national products; map of sources of energy.

**Politics and History** Map showing pre-colonial events, slave trade routes and areas of recent conflicts; timeline of important dates; map of European colonies in 1913; flag of the Organization of African Unity.

---

**Index** All the names on the maps and in the picture captions can be found in the index at the end of the book.

# CONTENTS

Chimpanzee
See page 17

# AFRICA

Africa, the second largest continent, is changing quickly. Around 50 years ago, European nations ruled most of Africa. As countries became independent, the new governments changed the way they were ruled and new names appeared on the map of Africa.

Many countries adopted one-party governments. Others suffered civil war and came under military dictators. Above all, Africa faces a struggle against poverty and many of its countries are among the world's poorest. Farming is the main activity, but many farmers produce little more than they need to support their families. Mining is important, but most of Africa lacks industries.

**Democracy** has been hard-won in many African countries. Nelson Mandela became president of South Africa in 1994. His 28 years in prison for his opposition to apartheid (a form of racial discrimination) in South Africa has made him an international symbol of liberty. He retired in 1999.

**People** South of the Sahara the continent is populated by black Africans, who speak more than 1,000 local languages. By contrast, in North Africa, the Arab and Berber people mostly speak Arabic. Disease and poverty are widespread and life expectancy is less than 50 years.

**Spectacular sights** attract an increasing number of tourists to Africa. The Victoria Falls, on the border between Zambia and Zimbabwe, is one of Africa's many scenic attractions. Local people call it Mosi-oa-tunya, or 'the smoke that thunders'.

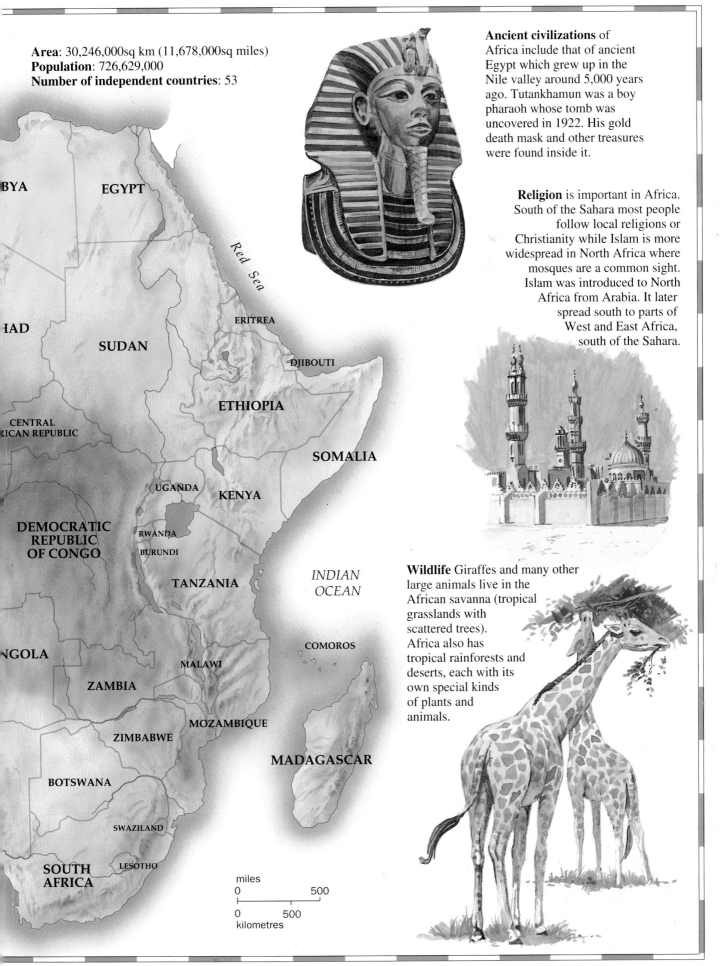

**Area**: 30,246,000sq km (11,678,000sq miles)
**Population**: 726,629,000
**Number of independent countries**: 53

**Ancient civilizations** of Africa include that of ancient Egypt which grew up in the Nile valley around 5,000 years ago. Tutankhamun was a boy pharaoh whose tomb was uncovered in 1922. His gold death mask and other treasures were found inside it.

**Religion** is important in Africa. South of the Sahara most people follow local religions or Christianity while Islam is more widespread in North Africa where mosques are a common sight. Islam was introduced to North Africa from Arabia. It later spread south to parts of West and East Africa, south of the Sahara.

**Wildlife** Giraffes and many other large animals live in the African savanna (tropical grasslands with scattered trees). Africa also has tropical rainforests and deserts, each with its own special kinds of plants and animals.

BYA
EGYPT
Red Sea
HAD
SUDAN
ERITREA
DJIBOUTI
ETHIOPIA
CENTRAL
RICAN REPUBLIC
SOMALIA
UGANDA
KENYA
DEMOCRATIC
REPUBLIC
OF CONGO
RWANDA
BURUNDI
INDIAN
OCEAN
TANZANIA
NGOLA
COMOROS
MALAWI
ZAMBIA
MOZAMBIQUE
ZIMBABWE
MADAGASCAR
BOTSWANA
SWAZILAND
SOUTH
AFRICA
LESOTHO

miles
0          500

0          500
kilometres

5

# NORTHWESTERN AFRICA

Northwestern Africa consists of three countries and one territory, called Western Sahara. Western Sahara was once ruled by Spain and called Spanish Sahara. It is now occupied by Morocco, but many of the local people have fought to make their country independent. The main regions of northwestern Africa are the fertile northern coasts, the high Atlas Mountains, which run through Morocco, Algeria and Tunisia, and the huge Sahara desert.

## ALGERIA

**Area**: 2,381,741sq km (919,595sq miles)
**Population**: 28,734,000
**Capital**: Algiers
**Largest cities**: Algiers (pop 1,772,000)
Oran (664,000)
Constantine (449,000)
**Official language**: Arabic
**Religions**: Islam
**Government**: Republic
**Currency**: Algerian dinar

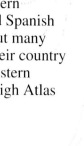

## MOROCCO

**Area**: 446,550sq km (172,414sq miles)
**Population**: 27,020,000
**Capital**: Rabat
**Largest cities**: Casablanca (pop 3,200,000)
Rabat (1,220,000)
Marrakesh (602,000)
**Official language**: Arabic
**Religions**: Islam
**Government**: Monarchy
**Currency**: Moroccan dirham

## TUNISIA

**Area**: 163,610sq km (63,170sq miles)
**Population**: 9,132,000
**Capital**: Tunis
**Largest cities**: Tunis (pop 674,000)
Sfax (231,000)
**Official language**: Arabic
**Religions**: Islam
**Government**: Republic
**Currency**: Tunisian dinar

## WESTERN SAHARA

**Area**: 266,000sq km (102,703sq miles)
**Population**: 287,000
**Government**: Status disputed, but occupied by Morocco.

**Atlas Mountains** These high ranges extend about 2,400km (1,490 miles) across Morocco, Algeria and northern Tunisia. The highest peak is Jebel Toubkal, in Morocco's High Atlas range.

*ATLANTIC OCEAN*

CANARY ISLANDS
(Spain)

Ceuta (S
**Tangier**
Kenitra
**Rabat** **Fez**
**Casablanca** Meknès

**MOROCCO**

**Marrakesh**
High Atlas
Toubkal
4165m
Agadir

G R A N

• Laâyoune

**Western Sahara**

Ad Dakhla •

**Leather goods**, such as purses, handbags, shoes and slippers, are made in Morocco. Other major crafts in northwestern Africa include the making of rugs, pottery and metal goods.

**Hassan II** became king of Morocco in 1961. Lesotho and Swaziland in southern Africa are also monarchies, but most African countries are republics. King Hassan heads the government of Morocco and has broad powers to make laws.

Mediterranean Sea

Annaba

**Algiers**   A t l a s   **Tunis**

Mostaganem   Tell   Constantine   Sousse

•Oran   M T S   •Batna   **TUNISIA**

ellila (Sp)   Saharan Atlas

jda   •Sfax

Ouargla

**A L G E R I A**

S A H A R A

D E S E R T

Ahaggar Mts

▲ Tahat 2918m

**Wine** is produced in the northern coastal regions of northwestern Africa. These regions have mild, moist winters and dry, sunny summers when the grapes ripen in the vineyards. Much of the wine is exported.

**Date palms** are common in North Africa. Dates, eaten fresh or dried, are an important food. The trunks and leaves of the tree are used in building, and the leaves are also used to make baskets and mats. The bark is used to make rope.

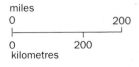

miles
0                    200

0            200
kilometres

**Oases** are places in deserts where there is enough water for plants to grow. Some oases in the Sahara, which makes up most of northwest Africa, get water from springs. Others tap underground water through wells.

# NORTHEASTERN AFRICA

The Nile valley was the home of Ancient Egypt, one of the world's earliest civilizations. Like its oil-rich neighbour Libya, it became part of the Roman Empire. Other ancient kingdoms developed in Sudan, Africa's largest country. Egypt has many factories, but farming is the main activity of the people in Sudan. The main religion of the region is Islam. In southern Sudan, where black Africans follow local religions or Christianity, many people have fought against rule by the Muslim north.

Tripoli
Misurata
Bengh

**LIBYA**

SAHARA DESERT

## EGYPT

**Area**: 1,001,449sq km (386,662sq miles)
**Population**: 59,272,000
**Capital**: Cairo
**Largest cities**: Cairo (pop 9,656,000)
Alexandria (3,380,000)
El Giza (2,144,000)
**Official language**: Arabic
**Religions**: Islam (90%), Christianity (10%)
**Government**: Republic
**Currency**: Egyptian pound

## LIBYA

**Area**: 1,759,540sq km (679,362sq miles)
**Population**: 5,167,000
**Capital**: Tripoli
**Largest cities**: Tripoli (pop 960,000)
Benghazi (472,000)
**Official language**: Arabic
**Religions**: Islam
**Government**: Republic
**Currency**: Libyan dinar

## SUDAN

**Area**: 2,505,813sq km (967,500sq miles)
**Population**: 27,272,000
**Capital**: Khartoum
**Largest cities**: Omdurman (pop 526,000)
Khartoum (476,000)
Khartoum North (341,000)
**Official language**: Arabic
**Religions**: Islam (72%), local religions (17%),
Christianity (11%)
**Government**: Republic
**Currency**: Sudanese dinar

**Oilfields** are found in the Sahara in central Libya. Pipelines carry the oil to the coast. Oil accounts for more than 90 per cent of Libya's exports. Egypt produces only enough oil for its own needs.

**Cotton** is the chief cash crop in Egypt and Sudan. Both produce textiles, including clothes. Egypt also manufactures food products and vehicles. It is Africa's second most important industrial country after South Africa.

**Colonel Muammar Gaddafi** and fellow military officers overthrew the king in Libya in 1969 and made Libya a republic. Gaddafi used money from oil exports to raise living standards in Libya. He has also given money to some overseas terrorist groups.

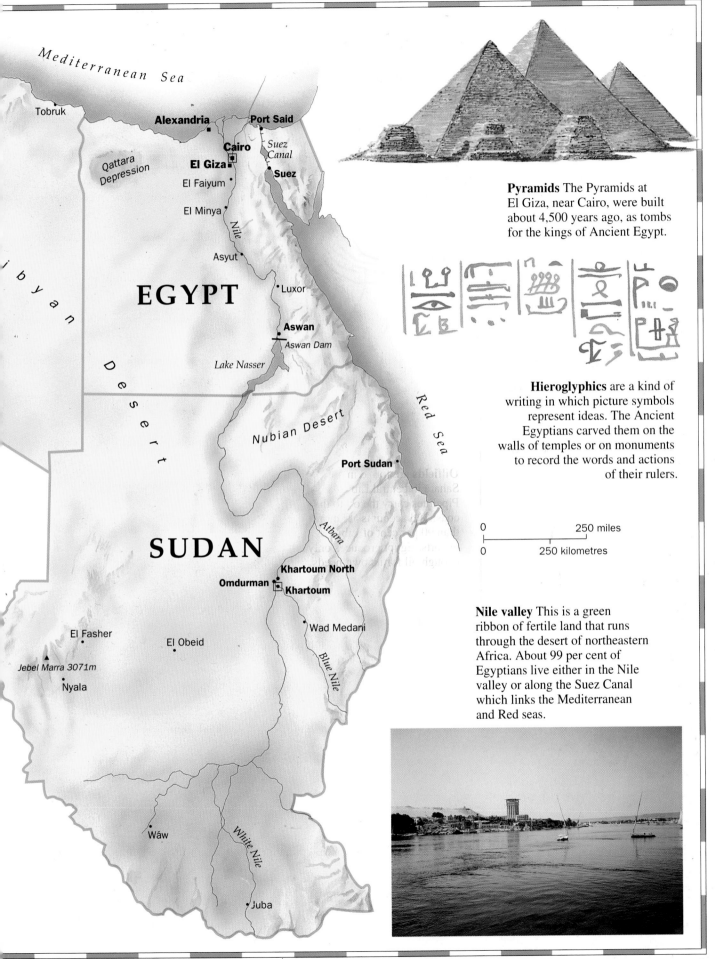

**Mediterranean Sea**

Tobruk

**Alexandria** • **Port Said**

Qattara
Depression

**Cairo**
*Suez
Canal*
**El Giza**
**Suez**

El Faiyum •

El Minya •

*Nile*

Asyut •

**EGYPT**

• Luxor

**Aswan**
*Aswan Dam*

*Lake Nasser*

*ibyan*

*Desert*

*Nubian Desert*

*Red Sea*

**Port Sudan** •

**SUDAN**

*Atbara*

El Fasher •

**Khartoum North**

**Omdurman** **Khartoum**

El Obeid •

• Wad Medani

▲ *Jebel Marra 3071m*

Nyala •

*Blue Nile*

• Wâw

*White Nile*

• Juba

**Pyramids** The Pyramids at
El Giza, near Cairo, were built
about 4,500 years ago, as tombs
for the kings of Ancient Egypt.

**Hieroglyphics** are a kind of
writing in which picture symbols
represent ideas. The Ancient
Egyptians carved them on the
walls of temples or on monuments
to record the words and actions
of their rulers.

```
0                    250 miles
0        250 kilometres
```

**Nile valley** This is a green
ribbon of fertile land that runs
through the desert of northeastern
Africa. About 99 per cent of
Egyptians live either in the Nile
valley or along the Suez Canal
which links the Mediterranean
and Red seas.

# HORN OF AFRICA

Four countries – Eritrea, Ethiopia, Djibouti and Somalia – are often called the Horn of Africa, because they resemble the shape of a rhinoceros horn on a map. Ethiopia is a mountainous country, with rainforests in the southwest. But the lands of northeastern and southeastern Ethiopia, Eritrea, Djibouti and Somalia are largely desert. All the countries are poor. They have suffered in recent years from droughts and civil wars.

## ERITREA

**Area**: 93,680sq km (36,170sq miles)
**Population**: 3,698,000
**Capital and largest city**: Asmara (pop 400,000)
**Official languages**: Tigrinya, Arabic
**Religions**: Islam (50%), Christianity (50%)
**Government**: Republic
**Currency**: Nakfa

## ETHIOPIA

**Area**: 1,128,220sq km (435,608sq miles)
**Population**: 58,234,000
**Capital and largest city**: Addis Ababa (pop 2,113,000)
**Official language**: None (Amharic is used in government)
**Religions**: Christianity (57%), Islam (31%), local religions (11%)
**Government**: Republic
**Currency**: Birr

## DJIBOUTI

**Area**: 22,000sq km (8,494sq miles)
**Population**: 619,000
**Capital and largest city**: Djibouti (pop 383,000)
**Official languages**: Arabic, French
**Religions**: Islam (97%)
**Government**: Republic
**Currency**: Djibouti franc

## SOMALIA

**Area**: 637,657sq km (246,201sq miles)
**Population**: 9,805,000
**Capital and largest city**: Mogadishu (pop 1,000,000)
**Official language**: Somali
**Religions**: Islam
**Government**: Republic
**Currency**: Somali shilling

**Haile Selassie I** was emperor of Ethiopia from 1930 until the monarchy was abolished in 1974. The military group that took over was overthrown in 1991 after a long civil war. Eritrea broke away from Ethiopia to become a separate country in 1993.

**Christianity** was introduced into Ethiopia in the 4th century. One of its best known churches, at Lalibela in northern Ethiopia, was carved out of solid rock in the 12th and 13th centuries.

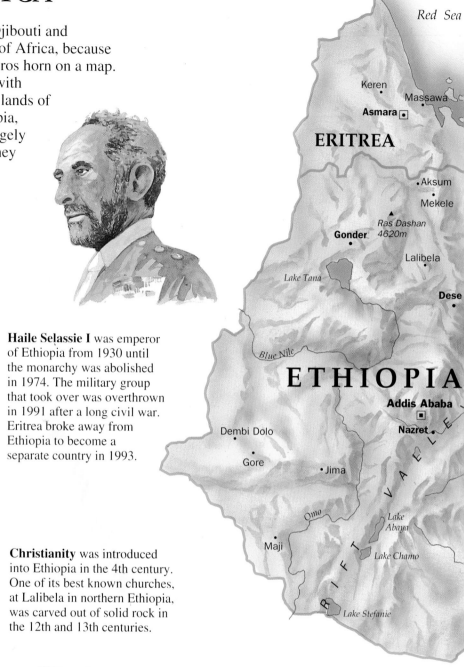

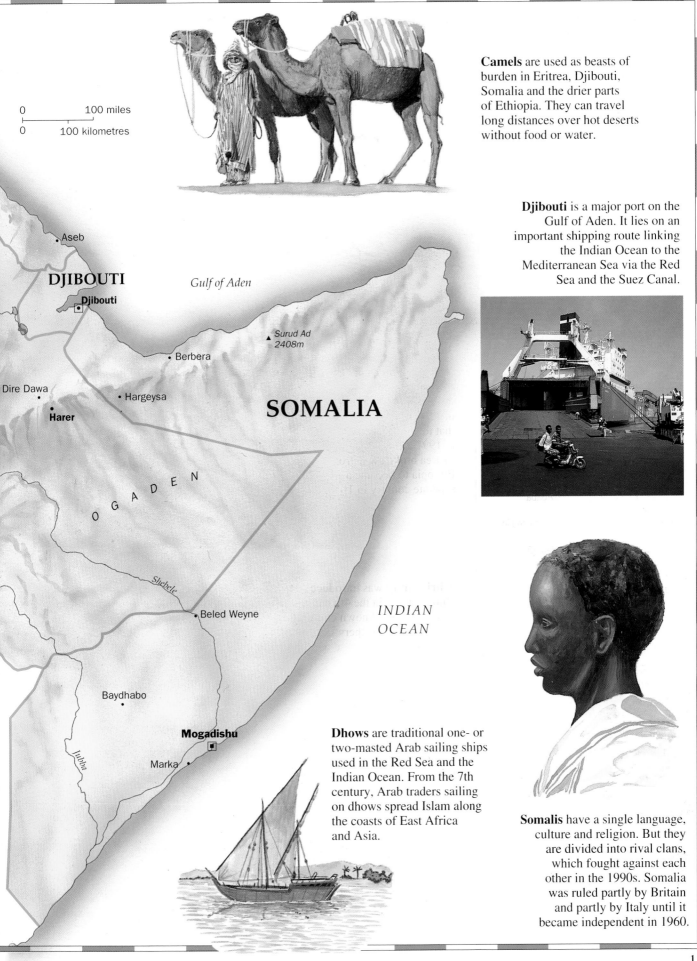

**Camels** are used as beasts of burden in Eritrea, Djibouti, Somalia and the drier parts of Ethiopia. They can travel long distances over hot deserts without food or water.

0 — 100 miles
0 — 100 kilometres

**Djibouti** is a major port on the Gulf of Aden. It lies on an important shipping route linking the Indian Ocean to the Mediterranean Sea via the Red Sea and the Suez Canal.

Aseb

**DJIBOUTI**

*Gulf of Aden*

Djibouti

▲ *Surud Ad 2408m*

Berbera

Dire Dawa

**Harer** • Hargeysa

**SOMALIA**

O G A D E N

*Shebele*

• Beled Weyne

*INDIAN OCEAN*

Baydhabo

*Jubba*

**Mogadishu**

Marka •

**Dhows** are traditional one- or two-masted Arab sailing ships used in the Red Sea and the Indian Ocean. From the 7th century, Arab traders sailing on dhows spread Islam along the coasts of East Africa and Asia.

**Somalis** have a single language, culture and religion. But they are divided into rival clans, which fought against each other in the 1990s. Somalia was ruled partly by Britain and partly by Italy until it became independent in 1960.

# WESTERN AFRICA 1

West Africa contains 15 countries (five of which are shown here). Desert covers much of Mauritania and Mali, but southern Mauritania and Mali, together with parts of Senegal and Burkina Faso, lie in a dry grassland region called the Sahel. To the south, the Sahel merges into savanna (tropical grassland with scattered trees). Forests grow along rivers. France once ruled Burkina Faso, Senegal, Mauritania and Mali. Gambia was ruled by Britain until 1965.

## MAURITANIA

**Area**: 1,030,700sq km (397,956sq miles)
**Population**: 2,332,000
**Capital and largest city**: Nouakchott (pop 600,000)
**Official language**: Arabic
**Religions**: Islam
**Government**: Islamic republic
**Currency**: Ouguiya

## MALI

**Area**: 1,240,000sq km (478,767sq miles)
**Population**: 9,999,000
**Capital and largest city**: Bamako (pop 746,000)
**Official language**: French
**Religions**: Islam (90%), local religions (9%), Christianity (1%)
**Government**: Republic
**Currency**: CFA franc*

## SENEGAL

**Area**: 196,192sq km (75,750sq miles)
**Population**: 8,534,000
**Capital and largest city**: Dakar (pop 1,729,000)
**Official language**: French
**Religions**: Islam 92%, local religions (6%), Christianity (2%)
**Government**: Republic
**Currency**: CFA franc

## GAMBIA

**Area**: 11,295sq km (4,361sq miles)
**Population**: 1,147,000
**Capital and largest city**: Banjul (pop 171,000)
**Official language**: English
**Religions**: Islam (96%), Christianity (4%)
**Government**: Republic
**Currency**: Dalasi

**Dakar** is the capital of Senegal. It is a major port with a fine harbour and is one of Africa's leading industrial cities. The French founded Dakar in 1857 on the site of a fishing village.

**Groundnuts** are among Gambia's and Senegal's leading exports. In the five countries on this page, more than 80 per cent of the people earn their living by farming.

## BURKINA FASO

**Area**: 274,200sq km (105,869sq miles)
**Population**: 10,669,000
**Capital and largest city**: Ouagadougou (pop 690,000)
**Official language**: French
**Religions**: Local religions (45%), Islam (43%), Christianity 12%
**Government**: Republic
**Currency**: CFA franc

\* CFA stands for Colonies Françaises d'Afrique

ATLANTIC OCEAN

• Nouadhibou

• Atâr

MAURITANIA

⊡ Nouakchott

• St Louis

**Dakar** ⊡

SENEGAL

• Thiès

• Kaolack

GAMBIA

Banjul ⊡

• Ziguinchor

Senegal

Gambia

S A

**Gambia** is a popular holiday spot for tourists from northern Europe. It has good beaches and interesting places to visit on cruises up the Gambia River.

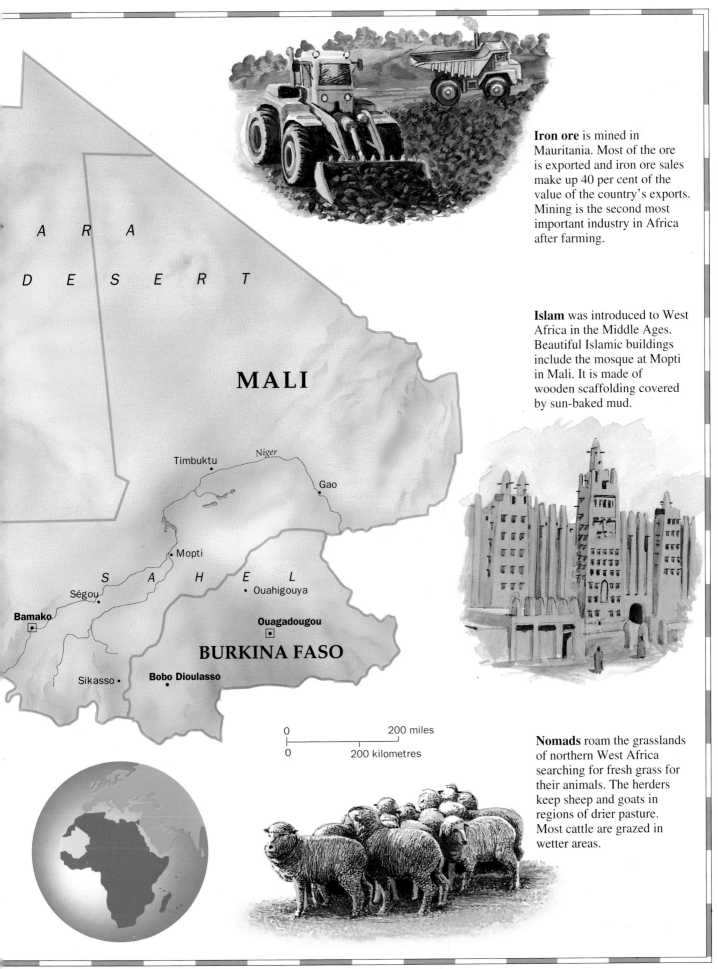

**Iron ore** is mined in Mauritania. Most of the ore is exported and iron ore sales make up 40 per cent of the value of the country's exports. Mining is the second most important industry in Africa after farming.

**Islam** was introduced to West Africa in the Middle Ages. Beautiful Islamic buildings include the mosque at Mopti in Mali. It is made of wooden scaffolding covered by sun-baked mud.

SAHARA DESERT

MALI

Timbuktu

Niger

Gao

Mopti

SAHEL

Ségou

Ouahigouya

Bamako

Ouagadougou

BURKINA FASO

Sikasso

Bobo Dioulasso

| 0 | 200 miles |
| 0 | 200 kilometres |

**Nomads** roam the grasslands of northern West Africa searching for fresh grass for their animals. The herders keep sheep and goats in regions of drier pasture. Most cattle are grazed in wetter areas.

# WESTERN AFRICA 2

The part of western Africa shown here includes four mainland countries and Cape Verde, a group of islands in the Atlantic Ocean, 640km (400 miles) west of Dakar, Liberia was founded by Americans in 1822 as a home for freed slaves and became independent in 1847. Guinea was ruled by France until 1958, Sierra Leone by Britain until 1961. Guinea-Bissau and Cape Verde were ruled by Portugal until the mid-1970s.

 **GUINEA**

**Area**: 245,857sq km (94,926sq miles)
**Population**: 6,759,000
**Capital and largest city**: Conakry (pop 1,508,000)
**Official language**: French
**Religions**: Islam (87%), local religions (5%), Christian (8%)
**Government**: Republic
**Currency**: Guinean franc

 **GUINEA-BISSAU**

**Area**: 36,125sq km (13,948sq miles)
**Population**: 1,094,000
**Capital and largest city**: Bissau (pop 145,000)
**Official language**: Portuguese
**Religions**: Local religions (54%), Islam (38%), Christianity (8%)
**Government**: Republic
**Currency**: CFA franc

 **SIERRA LEONE**

**Area**: 71,740sq km (27,699sq miles)
**Population**: 4,630,000
**Capital and largest city**: Freetown (pop 505,000)
**Official language**: English
**Religions**: Islam (60%), local religions (30%), Christianity (10%)
**Government**: Republic
**Currency**: Leone

 **LIBERIA**

**Area**: 111,369sq km (43,000sq miles)
**Population**: 2,810,000
**Capital and largest city**: Monrovia (pop 490,000)
**Official language**: English
**Religions**: Local religions (63%), Christianity (21%), Islam (16%)
**Government**: Republic
**Currency**: Liberian dollar

 **CAPE VERDE**

**Area**: 4,033sq km (1,557sq miles)
**Population**: 389,000
**Capital and largest city**: Praia (pop 69,000)
**Official language**: Portuguese
**Religions**: Christianity
**Government**: Republic
**Currency**: Escudo

CAPE VERDE

ATLANTIC OCEAN

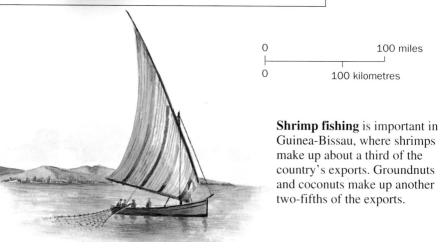

**Shrimp fishing** is important in Guinea-Bissau, where shrimps make up about a third of the country's exports. Groundnuts and coconuts make up another two-fifths of the exports.

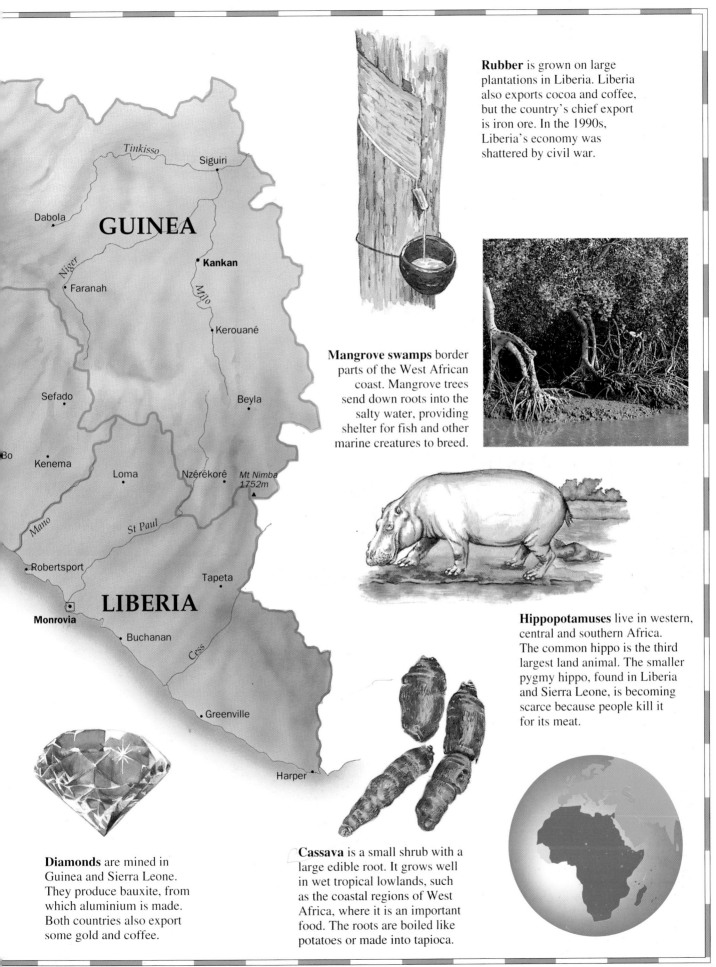

**Rubber** is grown on large plantations in Liberia. Liberia also exports cocoa and coffee, but the country's chief export is iron ore. In the 1990s, Liberia's economy was shattered by civil war.

GUINEA

Tinkisso

Siguiri

Dabola

Niger

Kankan

Faranah

Milo

Kerouané

Sefado

Beyla

Bo

Kenema

Loma

Nzérékoré

Mt Nimba 1752m

Mano

St Paul

Robertsport

Tapeta

LIBERIA

Monrovia

Buchanan

Cess

Greenville

Harper

**Mangrove swamps** border parts of the West African coast. Mangrove trees send down roots into the salty water, providing shelter for fish and other marine creatures to breed.

**Hippopotamuses** live in western, central and southern Africa. The common hippo is the third largest land animal. The smaller pygmy hippo, found in Liberia and Sierra Leone, is becoming scarce because people kill it for its meat.

**Diamonds** are mined in Guinea and Sierra Leone. They produce bauxite, from which aluminium is made. Both countries also export some gold and coffee.

**Cassava** is a small shrub with a large edible root. It grows well in wet tropical lowlands, such as the coastal regions of West Africa, where it is an important food. The roots are boiled like potatoes or made into tapioca.

# WESTERN AFRICA 3

Five countries make up the eastern part of West Africa. One of them, Nigeria, has more people than any other African country. Nigeria and Ghana were formerly British territories, while Benin, Côte d'Ivoire (Ivory Coast) and Togo were ruled by France. Nearly half of the people in this part of West Africa earn their living by farming. Cocoa, coconuts and palm products, coffee and cotton are leading exports. Nigeria's main export is oil.

**Cocoa beans**, from which chocolate is made, are grown in West Africa. Côte d'Ivoire and Ghana are the world's leading producers, while Nigeria ranks sixth. Other major products include coffee, cotton, palm oil and palm kernels.

## COTE D'IVOIRE

**Area**: 322,463sq km (124,504sq miles)
**Population**: 14,347,000
**Capital**: Yamoussoukro (pop 107,000)
**Largest city**: Abidjan (2,500,000)
**Official language**: French
**Religions**: Islam (39%), Christianity (26%), local religions (17%), other (18%)
**Government**: Republic
**Currency**: CFA franc

## GHANA

**Area**: 238,537sq km (92,100sq miles)
**Population**: 17,522,000
**Capital and largest city**: Accra (pop 1,781,000)
**Official language**: English
**Religions**: Local religions (38%), Islam (30%), Christianity (24%), other (8%)
**Government**: Republic
**Currency**: Cedi

## TOGO

**Area**: 56,785sq km (21,925sq miles)
**Population**: 4,230,000
**Capital and largest city**: Lomé (pop 590,000)
**Official language**: French
**Religions**: Local religions (50%), Christianity (35%), Islam (15%)
**Government**: Republic
**Currency**: CFA franc

## BENIN

**Area**: 112,622sq km (43,484sq miles)
**Population**: 5,632,000
**Capital**: Porto-Novo (pop 179,000)
**Largest city**: Cotonou (537,000)
**Official language**: French
**Religions**: Local religions (62%), Christianity (23%), Islam (12%), other (3%)
**Government**: Republic
**Currency**: CFA franc

## NIGERIA

**Area**: 923,768sq km (356,669sq miles)
**Population**: 114,568,000
**Capital**: Abuja (pop 339,000)
**Largest city**: Lagos (10,287,000)
**Official language**: English
**Religions**: Islam (51%), Christianity (40%), local religions (9%)
**Government**: Republic
**Currency**: Naira

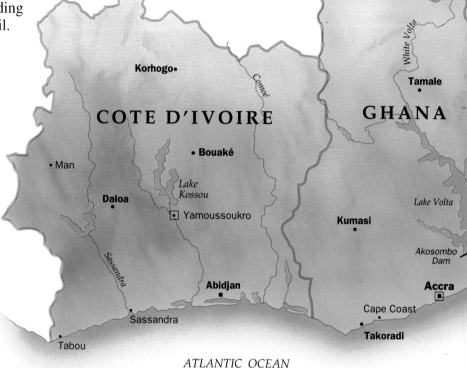

Korhogo

COTE D'IVOIRE

Tamale

GHANA

Bouaké

Man

Lake Kossou

Daloa

Yamoussoukro

Kumasi

Lake Volta

Sassandra

Akosombo Dam

Abidjan

Accra

Cape Coast

Sassandra

Takoradi

Tabou

*ATLANTIC OCEAN*

**Yamoussoukro**, capital of Côte d'Ivoire, has the world's largest church, the Basilica of Our Lady of Peace, which was completed in 1989. The city was the birthplace of Félix Houphouët-Boigny, the country's president (1960-93).

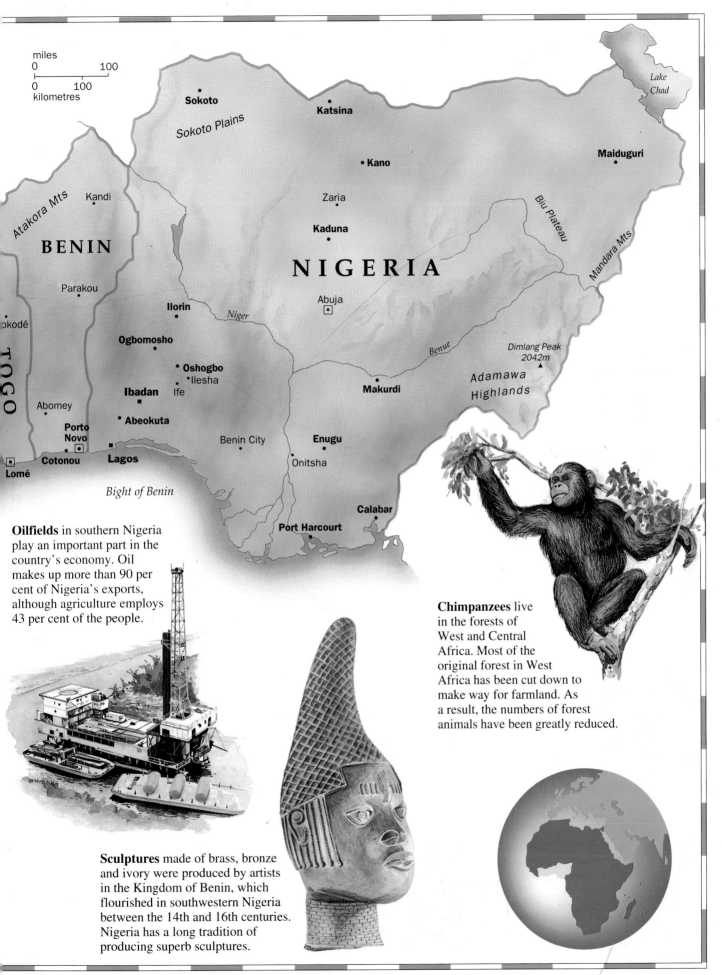

miles
0 — 100
0 — 100
kilometres

Sokoto

Sokoto Plains

Katsina

Kano

Maiduguri

Kandi

Atakora Mts

BENIN

Parakou

Zaria

Kaduna

Biu Plateau

NIGERIA

Mandara Mts

Ilorin

Niger

Abuja

Ogbomosho

Benue

Dimlang Peak
2042m

Oshogbo
Ilesha

Ibadan   Ife

Makurdi

Adamawa
Highlands

okodé

TOGO

Abomey

Abeokuta

Porto
Novo

Benin City

Enugu

Cotonou

Lagos

Onitsha

Lomé

Bight of Benin

Calabar

Port Harcourt

Lake
Chad

**Oilfields** in southern Nigeria play an important part in the country's economy. Oil makes up more than 90 per cent of Nigeria's exports, although agriculture employs 43 per cent of the people.

**Chimpanzees** live in the forests of West and Central Africa. Most of the original forest in West Africa has been cut down to make way for farmland. As a result, the numbers of forest animals have been greatly reduced.

**Sculptures** made of brass, bronze and ivory were produced by artists in the Kingdom of Benin, which flourished in southwestern Nigeria between the 14th and 16th centuries. Nigeria has a long tradition of producing superb sculptures.

# WEST-CENTRAL AFRICA

Bordering Nigeria are two huge landlocked nations, Chad and Niger. Although Niger has some mineral resources, these two countries are among the world's poorest. Both contain large areas of desert and dry grassland, and crops are grown only in the south. Central African Republic, another landlocked country south of Chad, has grasslands in the north and forests in the south. Agriculture employs 86 per cent of the people in this region.

## NIGER

**Area**: 1,267,000sq km (489,191sq miles)
**Population**: 9,335,000
**Capital**: Niamey (pop 398,000)
**Official language**: French
**Religions**: Islam (89%), local religions (11%)
**Government**: Republic
**Currency**: CFA franc

## CHAD

**Area**: 1,284,000sq km (495,755sq miles)
**Population**: 6,611,000
**Capital**: N'Djamena (pop 530,000)
**Official language**: French
**Religions**: Islam (54%), Christianity (35%), local religions (7%), other (4%)
**Government**: Republic
**Currency**: CFA franc

## CENTRAL AFRICAN REPUBLIC

**Area**: 622,984sq km (240,535sq miles)
**Population**: 3,344,000
**Capital**: Bangui (pop 706,000)
**Official language**: French
**Religions**: Local religions (57%), Christianity (35%), Islam (8%)
**Government**: Republic
**Currency**: CFA franc

**Deserts** cover most of northern Chad and Niger. To the south, the deserts merge into the dry, grassy Sahel: When severe droughts occur, the Sahel becomes desert. When the rains return, the Sahel becomes green again.

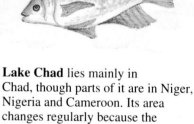

**Lake Chad** lies mainly in Chad, though parts of it are in Niger, Nigeria and Cameroon. Its area changes regularly because the amount of rainfall in west-central Africa varies from year to year. The lake is rich in fish. It is also a source of salt and potash.

**Niger** was named after the Niger, one of Africa's longest rivers, which flows through southwestern Niger. Its waters are used to irrigate farmland. Southern Niger and Chad are covered by savanna.

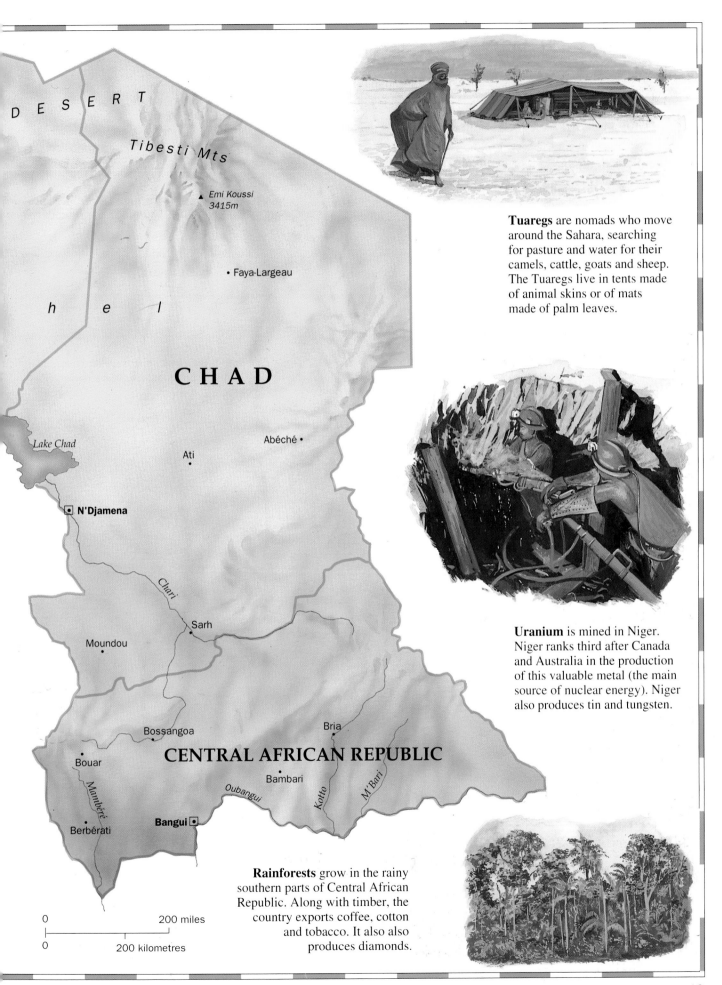

D E S E R T

Tibesti Mts

▲ Emi Koussi
3415m

• Faya-Largeau

h  e  l

CHAD

Lake Chad

Abéché •

Ati •

◼ N'Djamena

Chari

Sarh •

Moundou •

Bossangoa •

Bria •

**CENTRAL AFRICAN REPUBLIC**

Bouar •

Bambari •

Mambéré

Oubangui

Kotto

M'Bari

Berbérati •

**Bangui** ◉

0          200 miles

0          200 kilometres

**Tuaregs** are nomads who move around the Sahara, searching for pasture and water for their camels, cattle, goats and sheep. The Tuaregs live in tents made of animal skins or of mats made of palm leaves.

**Uranium** is mined in Niger. Niger ranks third after Canada and Australia in the production of this valuable metal (the main source of nuclear energy). Niger also produces tin and tungsten.

**Rainforests** grow in the rainy southern parts of Central African Republic. Along with timber, the country exports coffee, cotton and tobacco. It also also produces diamonds.

19

# CENTRAL AFRICA 1

Four tropical countries – Cameroon, Republic of Congo, Equatorial Guinea and Gabon – lie between Nigeria and the huge Democratic Republic of Congo. Equatorial Guinea contains an area on the mainland and a volcanic island, Bioko, which contains Gabon's capital. South of Bioko lies the island nation of São Tomé and Príncipe. Most people in these countries work on farms. Congo and Gabon have important oil deposits.

**Soccer** is a popular sport throughout Africa. National teams from Africa that have made their mark in international soccer competitions include Cameroon, Nigeria and Morocco.

## CAMEROON

**Area**: 475,442sq km (183,569sq miles)
**Population**: 13,676,000
**Capital**: Yaoundé (pop 649,000)
**Official languages**: English, French
**Religions**: Christianity (52%), local religions (26%), Islam (22%)
**Government**: Republic
**Currency**: CFA franc

## CONGO, REPUBLIC OF

**Area**: 342,000sq km (132,047sq miles)
**Population**: 2,705,000
**Capital**: Brazzaville (pop 938,000)
**Official language**: French
**Religions**: Christianity (65%), local religions (33%), Islam (2%)
**Government**: Republic
**Currency**: CFA franc

## EQUATORIAL GUINEA

**Area**: 28,051sq km (10,831sq miles)
**Population**: 410,000
**Capital**: Malabo (pop 35,000)
**Official languages**: Spanish, French
**Religions**: Christianity (89%), local religions (5%), other (6%)
**Government**: Republic
**Currency**: CFA franc

## GABON

**Area**: 267,667sq km (103,347sq miles)
**Population**: 1,125,000
**Capital**: Libreville (pop 418,000)
**Official language**: French
**Religions**: Christianity (80%), local religions (19%), Islam (1%)
**Government**: Republic
**Currency**: CFA franc

**Plantains** are a large kind of banana. They are grown throughout West and Central Africa, where they are eaten as a vegetable. The leaves are used to make bags or mats and sometimes for roofing houses.

## SAO TOME AND PRINCIPE

**Area**: 964sq km (372sq miles)
**Population**: 135,000
**Capital**: São Tomé (pop 43,000)
**Official language**: Portuguese
**Religions**: Christianity
**Government**: Republic
**Currency**: Dobra

*ATLANTIC OCEAN*

### SAO TOME AND PRINCIPE

São Tomé

*São Tomé*

*Annobón (Equat. Gui)*

**Libreville**, capital of Gabon, is a major port. Its name means 'free town', and its origins are similar to those of Liberia. Libreville was founded by French officers in 1849 as a home for freed slaves.

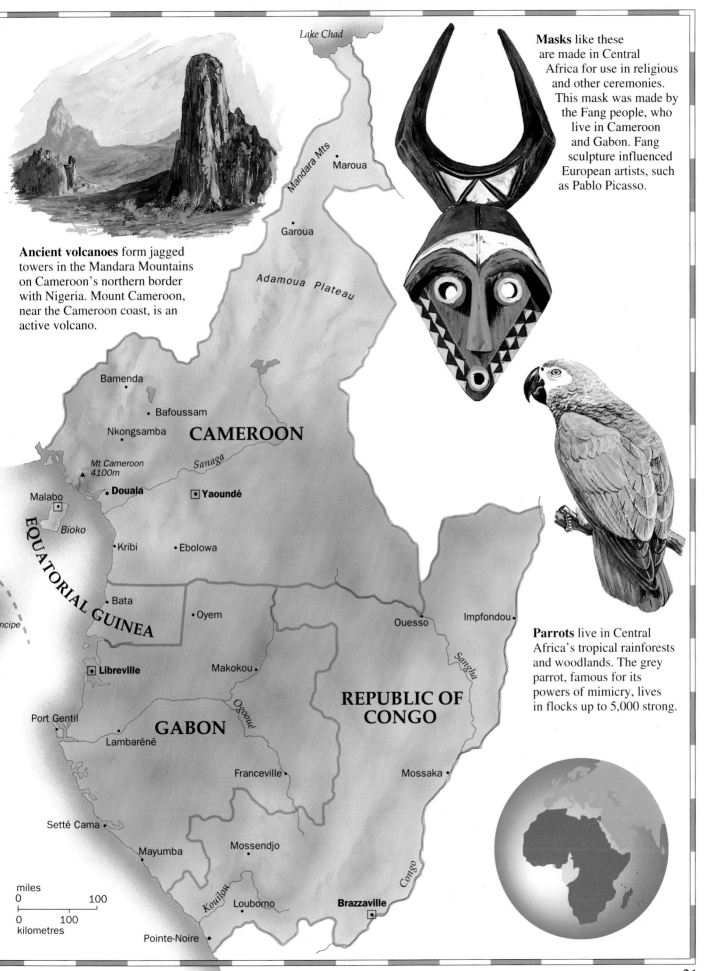

Lake Chad

Mandara Mts

Maroua

Garoua

Adamoua Plateau

**Ancient volcanoes** form jagged towers in the Mandara Mountains on Cameroon's northern border with Nigeria. Mount Cameroon, near the Cameroon coast, is an active volcano.

**Masks** like these are made in Central Africa for use in religious and other ceremonies. This mask was made by the Fang people, who live in Cameroon and Gabon. Fang sculpture influenced European artists, such as Pablo Picasso.

Bamenda

Bafoussam

Nkongsamba

**CAMEROON**

Mt Cameroon 4100m

**Douala**

Malabo

Bioko

**Yaoundé**

Sanaga

Kribi

Ebolowa

EQUATORIAL GUINEA

Bata

Oyem

Ouesso

Impfondou

Príncipe

Sangha

**Parrots** live in Central Africa's tropical rainforests and woodlands. The grey parrot, famous for its powers of mimicry, lives in flocks up to 5,000 strong.

**Libreville**

Makokou

**REPUBLIC OF CONGO**

Ogooué

Port Gentil

**GABON**

Lambaréné

Franceville

Mossaka

Setté Cama

Mayumba

Mossendjo

miles
0        100

0        100
kilometres

Kouilou

Loubomo

**Brazzaville**

Congo

Pointe-Noire

21

# CENTRAL AFRICA 2

The Democratic Republic of Congo, called Zaire from 1971 to 1997, is Africa's third largest country after Sudan and Algeria. It was ruled by Belgium until 1960, when the country was plunged into civil war between rival ethnic groups. The army leader General Mobutu restored order, but he became a dictator. Mobutu was overthrown in 1997. Burundi and Rwanda have also suffered civil wars between two groups, the Hutus and Tutsis.

## DEMOCRATIC REPUBLIC OF CONGO

**Area**: 2,345,409sq km (905,568sq miles)
**Population**: 45,234,000
**Capital**: Kinshasa
**Largest cities**: Kinshasa (pop 4,655,000)
Lubumbashi (851,000)
Mbuji Mayi (806,000)
**Official language**: French
**Religions**: Christianity (87%), local religions (12%), Islam (1%)
**Government**: Military regime
**Currency**: Congo franc

## BURUNDI

**Area**: 27,834sq km (10,747sq miles)
**Population**: 6,423,000
**Capital**: Bujumbura (pop 235,000)
**Official languages**: Rundi, French
**Government**: Republic (military regime)
**Currency**: Burundi franc

## RWANDA

**Area**: 26,338sq km (10,169sq miles)
**Population**: 6,727,000
**Capital**: Kigali (pop 232,000)
**Official language**: Kinyarwanda, French
**Government**: Republic
**Currency**: Rwanda franc

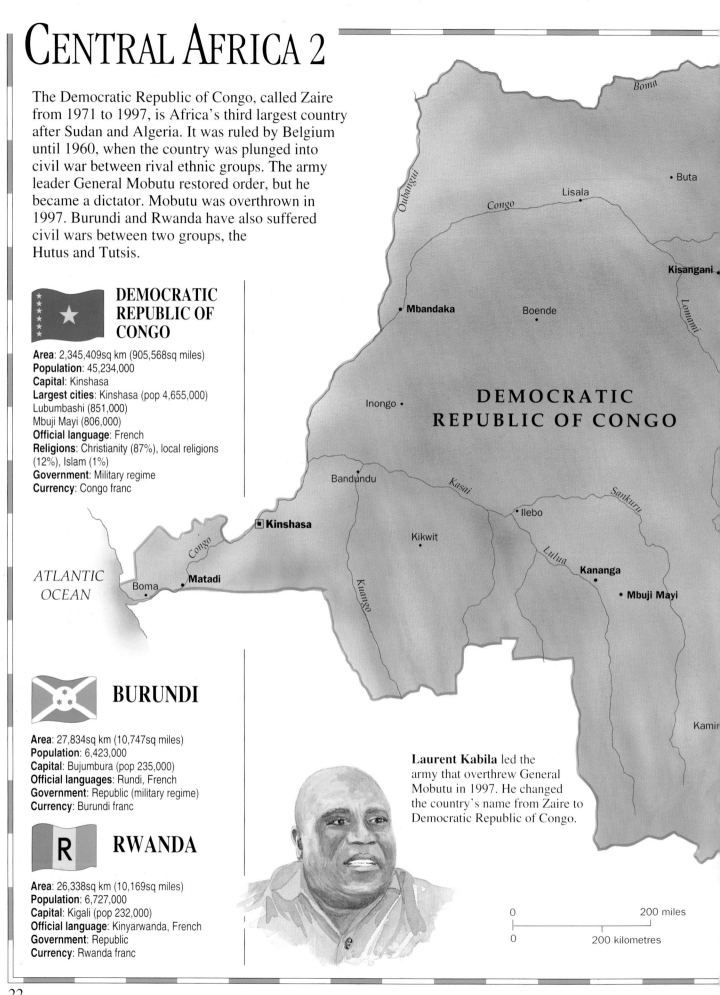

**Laurent Kabila** led the army that overthrew General Mobutu in 1997. He changed the country's name from Zaire to Democratic Republic of Congo.

0    200 miles

0    200 kilometres

**Congo** is also the name of the world's fifth longest river. Called the Zaire from 1971-97, the river has more water than any other apart from the Amazon in South America. It is a major route for carrying goods through the dense rainforest.

**Pygmies** live in small groups in the forests of Central Africa. From around 100 BC, people from the Cameroon area, who spoke Bantu languages, began to settle in Central Africa. They pushed the Pygmies into remote areas. Bantu-speaking people now occupy most of Central, East and Southern Africa.

**Mountain gorillas** live in Rwanda and in the mountains to the west. Their survival in Rwanda was threatened in the 1990s by fighting in the area where they live. Conflict between Hutus and Tutsis caused great loss of life and harmed the economies of Burundi and Rwanda.

**Mining** is a major industry in the Democratic Republic of Congo, which leads the world in mining industrial diamonds. It also produces copper, cobalt, manganese, silver and tin. Some oil is obtained off the coast.

**Coffee** dominates the exports of both Burundi and Rwanda. The two war-shattered countries rank among the ten poorest in the world. Manufacturing and mining are on a small scale.

Isiro

*Aruwimi*

Lake Albert

Margherita Peak 5110m

Lake Edward

**RWANDA**

Lake Kivu

⊡ **Kigali**

**Bukavu** •

• Kindu

**Bujumbura**
⊡

**BURUNDI**

*Lualaba*

Lake Tanganyika

*M i t u m b a   M t s*

Kabalo

Kalemie •

Lake Mweru

*K a t a n g a*

Likasi
•wezi •

**Lubumbashi**
•

# EAST AFRICA

East Africa consists of three countries that were formerly ruled by Britain. Although the region lies on the equator, much of it is high tableland and the weather is much more pleasant than on the hot and humid coast. All three countries have large national parks, where visitors can see a wide variety of wildlife at close range. More than 80 per cent of the people live by farming. The main products include coffee, cotton and tea.

## UGANDA

**Area**: 236,036sq km (91,134sq miles)
**Population**: 19,741,000
**Capital**: Kampala (pop 874,000)
**Official languages**: Swahili, English
**Religions**: Christianity (65%), local religions (19%), Islam (15%), other (1%)
**Government**: Republic
**Currency**: Uganda shilling

## KENYA

**Area**: 582,646sq km (224,961sq miles)
**Population**: 27,364,000
**Capital**: Nairobi (pop 1,505,000)
**Official languages**: Swahili, English
**Religions**: Christianity (73%), local religions (19%), Islam (6%), other (2%)
**Government**: Republic
**Currency**: Kenyan shilling

## TANZANIA

**Area**: 945,087sq km (364,900sq miles)
**Population**: 30,494,000
**Capital**: Dodoma (pop 204,000)
**Official languages**: Swahili, English
**Religions**: Islam (35%), local religions (35%), Christianity (30%)
**Government**: Republic
**Currency**: Tanzania shilling

**Lake Victoria** is Africa's largest lake and also the world's second largest freshwater lake after Lake Superior in North America. One of the main sources of the River Nile, it was named after Queen Victoria.

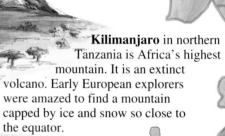

**Kilimanjaro** in northern Tanzania is Africa's highest mountain. It is an extinct volcano. Early European explorers were amazed to find a mountain capped by ice and snow so close to the equator.

**Serengeti National Park**, in northern Tanzania, covers 14,500sq km (5,600sq miles). It contains many animals, such as zebras, buffaloes, elephants, gazelles, giraffes, leopards and lions. Many tourists visit East Africa to see the wonderful wildlife.

**Olduvai Gorge** is a site in northern Tanzania where the fossils of ancient human-like creatures have been found, together with the tools they used. Many scientists believe that the first true humans evolved in East Africa.

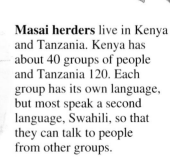

**Masai herders** live in Kenya and Tanzania. Kenya has about 40 groups of people and Tanzania 120. Each group has its own language, but most speak a second language, Swahili, so that they can talk to people from other groups.

Gulu

Nile

Masindi

Lake Albert

Kabarole

Entebbe

Lake Edward

Bukoba

Ujiji

Lake Tanganyika

Lake Rukwa

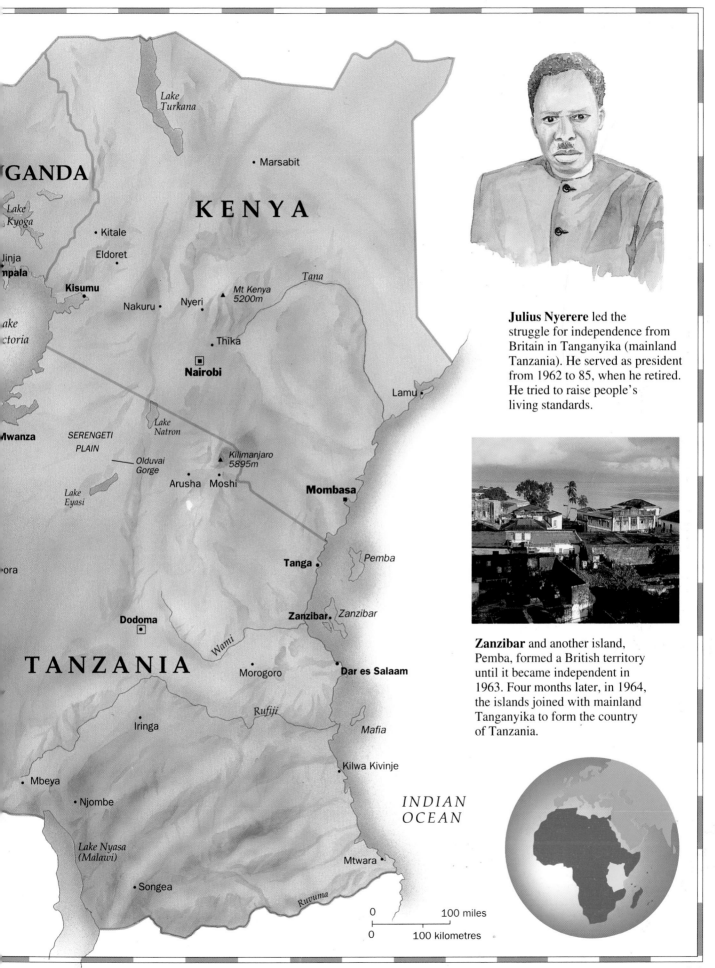

UGANDA

KENYA

Lake Turkana

• Marsabit

Lake Kyoga

• Kitale

Eldoret

Jinja

mpala

**Kisumu**

Nakuru • • Nyeri

▲ Mt Kenya 5200m

*Tana*

• Thika

**Nairobi**

Lamu •

ake ctoria

Mwanza

*SERENGETI PLAIN*

*Lake Natron*

*Olduvai Gorge*

▲ *Kilimanjaro 5895m*

*Lake Eyasi*

Arusha  Moshi

**Mombasa**

ora

**Tanga** •

*Pemba*

**Dodoma**

**Zanzibar**• *Zanzibar*

**TANZANIA**

*Wami*

Morogoro •

**Dar es Salaam**

*Rufiji*

Iringa •

*Mafia*

• Kilwa Kivinje

• Mbeya

*INDIAN OCEAN*

• Njombe

*Lake Nyasa (Malawi)*

Mtwara •

• Songea

*Ruvuma*

**Julius Nyerere** led the struggle for independence from Britain in Tanganyika (mainland Tanzania). He served as president from 1962 to 85, when he retired. He tried to raise people's living standards.

**Zanzibar** and another island, Pemba, formed a British territory until it became independent in 1963. Four months later, in 1964, the islands joined with mainland Tanganyika to form the country of Tanzania.

| 0 | 100 miles |
| 0 | 100 kilometres |

# INDIAN OCEAN TERRITORIES

Four independent island countries in the Indian Ocean are considered to be part of the African continent. They are Madagascar, which is by far the largest, Comoros, Mauritius and Seychelles. The French island of Réunion, east of Madagascar, is also part of Africa. Madagascar is unusual. Its people are a mixture of Indonesian and black African people. Its chief language, Malagasy, resembles Malay and Indonesian.

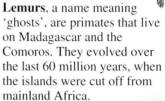

**Lemurs**, a name meaning 'ghosts', are primates that live on Madagascar and the Comoros. They evolved over the last 60 million years, when the islands were cut off from mainland Africa.

## SEYCHELLES

**Area:** 404sq km (156sq miles)
**Population:** 77,000
**Capital:** Victoria (pop 30,000)
**Official language:** None
**Religions:** Christianity (96%), Hinduism (1%), other (3%)
**Government:** Republic
**Currency:** Seychelles rupee

## COMOROS

**Area:** 2,171sq km (838sq miles)
**Population:** 505,000
**Capital:** Moroni (pop 22,000)
**Official languages:** Comorian, Arabic, French
**Religions:** Islam (99%), Christianity (1%)
**Government:** Islamic republic
**Currency:** Comorian franc

## MADAGASCAR

**Area:** 587,041sq km (226,658sq miles)
**Population:** 13,705,000
**Capital:** Antananarivo (pop 1,053,000)
**Official language:** Malagasy
**Religions:** Local religions (52%), Christianity (41%), Islam (7%)
**Government:** Republic
**Currency:** Malagasy franc

**Spices** are grown on Indian Ocean islands. The Comoros, a producer of cloves, vanilla and perfume oils, became independent in 1975. Two of the three islands tried to break away from the country in 1997-98.

## MAURITIUS

**Area:** 1,865sq km (720sq miles)
**Population:** 1,134,000
**Capital:** Port Louis (pop 146,000)
**Official language:** English
**Religions:** Hinduism (51%), Christianity (32%), Islam (16%), other (1%)
**Government:** Republic
**Currency:** Mauritian rupee

## REUNION

### (French overseas department)

**Area:** 2,510sq km (969sq miles)
**Population:** 664,000
**Capital:** Saint-Denis (pop 104,000)
**Official language:** French
**Religions:** Christianity (94%), other (6%)
**Currency:** French franc

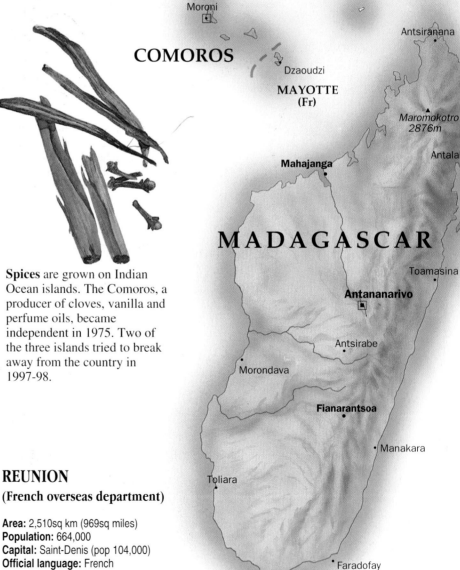

Aldabra

SEYC

Moroni

Antsiranana

COMOROS

Dzaoudzi

MAYOTTE
(Fr)

Maromokotro
2876m

Antalah

Mahajanga

MADAGASCAR

Toamasina

Antananarivo

Antsirabe

Morondava

Fianarantsoa

Manakara

Toliara

Faradofay

Victoria
Mahé

L L E S

INDIAN OCEAN

**Turtles**, like this leatherback, come on shore in the Seychelles and other islands to lay their eggs. Hunted for food and for their shells, they are now an endangered species – though there are no reliable records of their numbers.

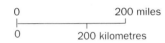

```
0          200 miles
0          200 kilometres
```

**Tourism** is the chief activity of people in the Seychelles, which has many beautiful beaches. Tourism is also important on other islands, especially Mauritius and Madagascar.

**Rice** is the chief food crop in Madagascar. Historians believe that rice-growing was introduced to Madagascar by people from Southeast Asia who settled on the island. Coffee is Madagascar's leading export.

**MAURITIUS**

Port Louis

Saint-Denis

**REUNION (Fr)**

**Sugar cane** is the leading crop and one of the chief exports of Mauritius. Most of it is grown on large plantations. Sugar production employs about one-third of all workers on the island.

27

# SOUTHEASTERN AFRICA

Southeastern Africa consists of two former British territories – Malawi and Swaziland – and the former Portuguese territory of Mozambique. Malawi became independent in 1964 and Swaziland in 1968. Mozambique achieved independence in 1975. A civil war then occurred as a rebel force, supported by the white governments in Rhodesia (now Zimbabwe) and South Africa, fought to overthrow the government. Many people died. The civil war in Mozambique officially ended in 1992.

## MALAWI

**Area**: 118,484sq km (45,747sq miles)
**Population**: 10,016,000
**Capital**: Lilongwe (pop 234,000)
**Official languages**: Chichewa, English
**Religions**: Christianity (50%), Islam (20%), local religions (10%), other (20%)
**Government**: Republic
**Currency**: Kwacha

## MOZAMBIQUE

**Area**: 801,590sq km (309,496sq miles)
**Population**: 18,028,000
**Capital**: Maputo (pop 934,000)
**Official language**: Portuguese
**Religions**: Local religions (48%), Christianity (39%), Islam (13%)
**Government**: Republic
**Currency**: Metical

## SWAZILAND

**Area**: 17,363sq km (6,704sq miles)
**Population**: 926,000
**Capital**: Mbabane (pop 38,000)
**Official languages**: Swazi, English
**Religions**: Christianity (77%), local religions (21%), other (2%)
**Government**: Monarchy
**Currency**: Lilangeni

**Hastings Kamuzu Banda** led the independence struggle in Malawi. After independence in 1964, he became prime minister and later president, but he became increasingly arrogant, suppressing all opposition. He was defeated in elections in 1994 and died in 1997.

**Lake Malawi** occupies part of the Great Rift Valley. This deep valley runs from southeastern Africa, through East Africa and Ethiopia to the Red Sea. It continues into southwestern Asia, where it contains the Dead Sea.

**Hydroelectricity** is produced at the Cabora Bassa Dam on the Zambezi River in western Mozambique. Coal and oil are in short supply in much of southern Africa. Hydroelectric plants are major sources of electricity.

**Pineapples** are an important crop in Swaziland, together with citrus fruits, cotton, rice, sugar cane and tobacco. Swaziland has a varied economy. It is one of the few countries in Africa that exports more than it imports.

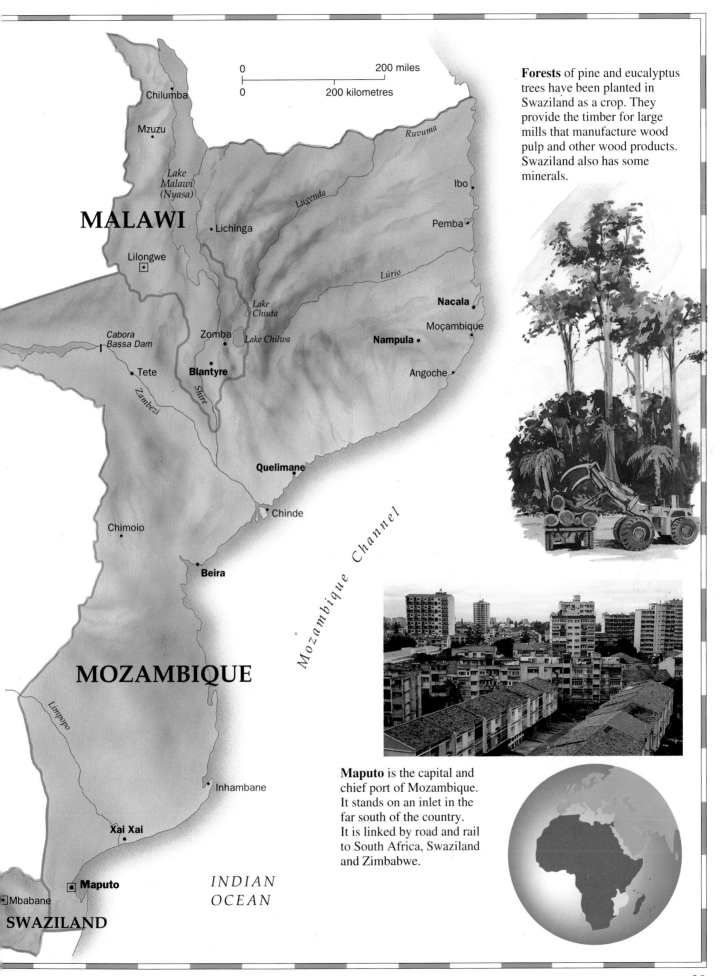

**MALAWI**

Chilumba

Mzuzu

*Lake Malawi (Nyasa)*

Lichinga

*Ruvuma*

*Lugenda*

Ibo

Pemba

Lilongwe

*Lúrio*

**Nacala**

Lake Chiuta

Zomba

Lake Chilwa

Moçambique

**Nampula**

*Cabora Bassa Dam*

Tete

**Blantyre**

Angoche

*Zambezi*

*Shire*

**Quelimane**

Chinde

Chimoio

*Mozambique Channel*

**Beira**

**MOZAMBIQUE**

*Limpopo*

Inhambane

**Xai Xai**

*INDIAN OCEAN*

■ **Maputo**

•Mbabane

**SWAZILAND**

0      200 miles

0      200 kilometres

**Forests** of pine and eucalyptus trees have been planted in Swaziland as a crop. They provide the timber for large mills that manufacture wood pulp and other wood products. Swaziland also has some minerals.

**Maputo** is the capital and chief port of Mozambique. It stands on an inlet in the far south of the country. It is linked by road and rail to South Africa, Swaziland and Zimbabwe.

# SOUTH-CENTRAL AFRICA

Two large landlocked countries – Zambia and Zimbabwe – lie at the heart of southern Africa. Zambia is a former British territory that was called Northern Rhodesia before it became independent in 1964. Zimbabwe, another former British territory, was formerly called Southern Rhodesia and then, from 1964 to 1980, Rhodesia. Both countries have important mineral resources. But agriculture still employs about 70 per cent of the people.

**Beef cattle** are reared on large ranches in Zimbabwe. Dairy cattle are also important and milk is a major product. Maize is the chief food crop in both Zimbabwe and Zambia.

## ZAMBIA

**Area**: 752,614sq km (290,586sq miles)
**Population**: 9,215,000
**Capital**: Lusaka
**Largest cities**: Lusaka (pop 921,000)
Kitwe (495,000)
Ndola (467,000)
Kabwe (210,000)
Mufulira (206,000)
**Official language**: English
**Religions**: Christianity (72%), local religions (27%), other (1%)
**Government**: Republic
**Currency**: Kwacha

## ZIMBABWE

**Area**: 390,580sq km (150,804sq miles)
**Population**: 11,248,000
**Capital**: Harare
**Largest cities**: Harare (pop 1,184,000)
Bulawayo (621,000)
Chitungwiza (274,000)
Mutare (132,000)
Gweru (125,000)
**Official language**: English
**Religions**: Christianity (45%), local religions (40%), others (15%)
**Government**: Republic
**Currency**: Zimbabwe dollar

**Copper** is mined in a region called the Copperbelt in northern Zambia, along the border with the Democratic Republic of Congo. Copper accounts for about 70 per cent of Zambia's exports.

**Great Zimbabwe** is a historic site in Zimbabwe that contains the ruins of impressive stone buildings. It was capital of a Shona kingdom that flourished between the Limpopo and Zambezi rivers between about 1250 and 1450.

Kasempa

Zambezi

Mongu

Sesheke

Livingstor

Victoria
Falls

**Tobacco** is a major export from Zimbabwe and the country ranks sixth among the world's tobacco producers. Zimbabwe also exports maize and cotton. Zambia also produces some tobacco.

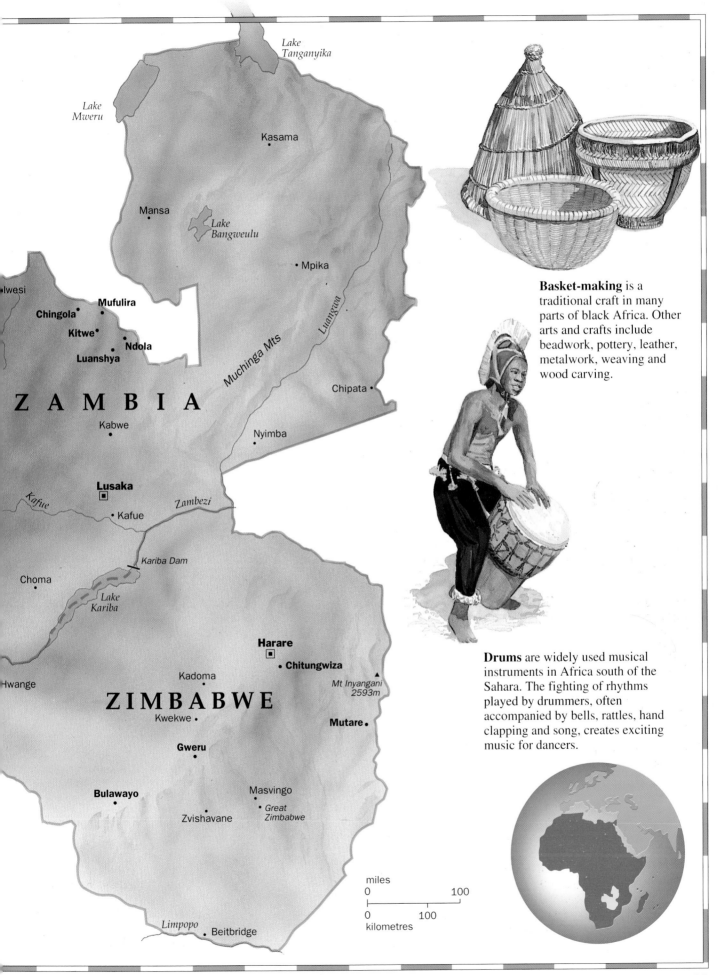

Lake
Tanganyika

Lake
Mweru

Kasama

Mansa

Lake
Bangweulu

Mpika

Iwesi

Mufulira

Chingola

Kitwe

Ndola

Luanshya

Luangwa

Muchinga Mts

Chipata

**ZAMBIA**

Kabwe

Nyimba

**Lusaka**

Kafue

Zambezi

Kafue

Kariba Dam

Choma

Lake
Kariba

**Harare**

Chitungwiza

Kadoma

Mt Inyangani
2593m

Hwange

**ZIMBABWE**

Kwekwe

Mutare

**Gweru**

Masvingo

**Bulawayo**

Great
Zimbabwe

Zvishavane

Limpopo

Beitbridge

miles

0                    100

0            100

kilometres

**Basket-making** is a
traditional craft in many
parts of black Africa. Other
arts and crafts include
beadwork, pottery, leather,
metalwork, weaving and
wood carving.

**Drums** are widely used musical
instruments in Africa south of the
Sahara. The fighting of rhythms
played by drummers, often
accompanied by bells, rattles, hand
clapping and song, creates exciting
music for dancers.

# SOUTHWESTERN AFRICA

Southwestern Africa consists of Angola and Namibia on the Atlantic Ocean coast, and Botswana, a landlocked country that borders Namibia. Botswana is a former British territory that became independent in 1966. Angola became independent from Portugal in 1975, but it then suffered a long civil war. Namibia, formerly called South West Africa, became independent from South Africa in 1990.

**Maize** is an important part of the diet of many black Africans in southern Africa. It contains starch, which provides the body with energy, but it lacks many other nutrients the body needs. People who depend on it may suffer from malnutrition.

 **ANGOLA**

**Area:** 1,246,700sq km (481,354sq miles)
**Population:** 11,100,000
**Capital:** Luanda (pop 2,250,000)
**Official language:** Portuguese
**Religions:** Christianity (70%), local religions (30%)
**Government:** Republic
**Currency:** Kwanza

 **BOTSWANA**

**Area:** 581,730sq km (224,607sq miles)
**Population:** 1,480,000
**Capital:** Gaborone (pop 133,000)
**Official language:** English, Setswana
**Religions:** Christianity (50%), local religions (49%), other (1%)
**Government:** Republic
**Currency:** Pula

 **NAMIBIA**

**Area:** 824,292sq km (318,261sq miles)
**Population:** 1,584,000
**Capital:** Windhoek (pop 126,000)
**Official language:** English
**Religions:** Christianity (82%), other (18%)
**Government:** Republic
**Currency:** Namibian dollar

**Wood carving** is one of the leading art forms in black Africa. Carvings of chiefs and heroes by the Chokwe people of Angola, made over the last 200 years, are found in museums all round the world. But wood is perishable and few older carvings have survived.

**Sand dunes** form towering hills in the Namib Desert, which stretches along the western coast of Namibia. Most of the little water it gets comes from mists that roll in from the sea.

CABINDA
(Angola)
Cabinda

Luanda
Cuanza
Malanje

**ANGOLA**

Lobito
Serra Moco
2619m
Benguela
Huambo

Namibe
Lubango
Cubango

Cunene

Etosha Pan

N
a
m
i
b

Otjiwarongo

ATLANTIC
OCEAN

**NAMIBIA**

Windhoek

Walvis Bay

D
e
s
e
r
t

Lüderitz

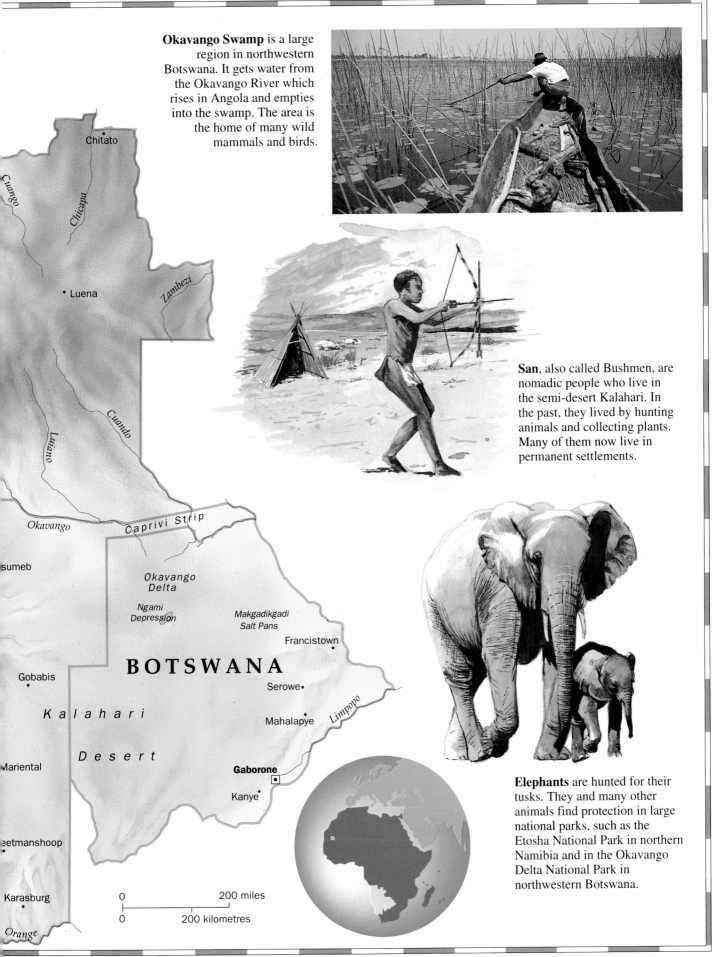

**Okavango Swamp** is a large region in northwestern Botswana. It gets water from the Okavango River which rises in Angola and empties into the swamp. The area is the home of many wild mammals and birds.

**San**, also called Bushmen, are nomadic people who live in the semi-desert Kalahari. In the past, they lived by hunting animals and collecting plants. Many of them now live in permanent settlements.

**Elephants** are hunted for their tusks. They and many other animals find protection in large national parks, such as the Etosha National Park in northern Namibia and in the Okavango Delta National Park in northwestern Botswana.

Chitato

Cuango

Chicapa

Luena

Zambezi

Cuando

Luiano

Okavango

Caprivi Strip

sumeb

Okavango Delta

Ngami Depression

Makgadikgadi Salt Pans

Francistown

**BOTSWANA**

Gobabis

Serowe•

K a l a h a r i

Mahalapye

Limpopo

D e s e r t

Mariental

**Gaborone**

Kanye•

eetmanshoop

Karasburg

Orange

0        200 miles

0        200 kilometres

# SOUTHERN AFRICA

South Africa and Lesotho occupy the southern tip of Africa. South Africa is Africa's most developed country, though most of its black people are poor. In 1948, the South African government introduced a policy called apartheid, under which non-whites had no votes and strictly limited human rights. But multiracial elections in 1994 produced a government and equal rights for all the people of South Africa.

**Gold mining** is important in South Africa, which leads the world in gold production. The country also produces coal, chromite, copper, diamonds, iron ore, manganese, platinum and uranium. South Africa is also the most industrialized country in the continent.

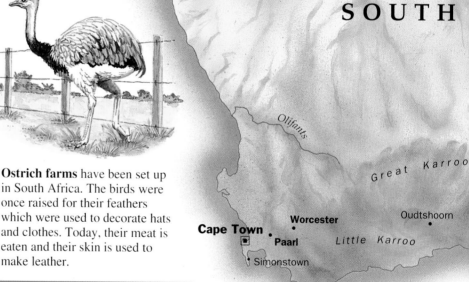

## SOUTH AFRICA

**Area:** 1,221,037sq km (471,445sq miles)
**Population:** 37,643,000
**Capitals:** Pretoria (administrative), Cape Town (legislative), Bloemfontein (judicial)
**Largest cities:** Cape Town (pop 2,350,000)
Johannesburg (1,196,000)
Durban (1,137,000)
Pretoria (1,080,000)
Port Elizabeth (853,000)
**Official languages:** Afrikaans, English, Ndebele, North Sotho, South Sotho, Swazi, Tsonga, Tswana, Venda, Xhosa, Zulu
**Religions:** Christianity (66%), local religions (30%), Hinduism (1%), Islam (1%), other (2%)
**Government:** Republic
**Currency:** Rand

## LESOTHO

**Area:** 30,355sq km (11,720sq miles)
**Population:** 2,023,000
**Capital:** Maseru (pop 109,000)
**Official languages:** Sesotho, English
**Religions:** Christianity (93%), local religions (7%)
**Government:** Monarchy
**Currency:** Loti

**Ostrich farms** have been set up in South Africa. The birds were once raised for their feathers which were used to decorate hats and clothes. Today, their meat is eaten and their skin is used to make leather.

**Table Mountain** is a flat-topped upland which overlooks Cape Town and Table Bay, in southwestern South Africa. Cloud often covers the top of Table Mountain and spills over the edge like a tablecloth.

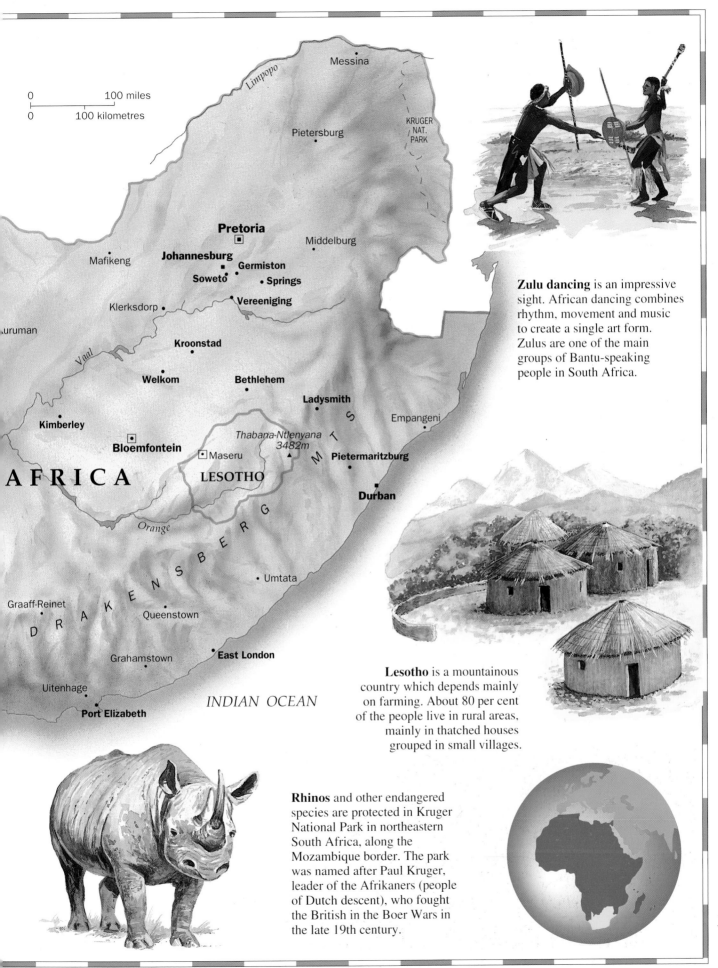

Messina

*Limpopo*

0 —— 100 miles
0 —— 100 kilometres

Pietersburg

KRUGER
NAT.
PARK

**Pretoria**

Middelburg

Mafikeng

**Johannesburg**
 • **Germiston**
**Soweto**
 • **Springs**

Klerksdorp •

 • **Vereeniging**

uruman

*Vaal*

**Kroonstad**

**Welkom**

**Bethlehem**

**Kimberley**

**Ladysmith**

Empangeni

*Thabana-Ntlenyana*
*3482m*

**Bloemfontein**

▣ Maseru

▲

**Pietermaritzburg**

**A F R I C A**

**LESOTHO**

*Orange*

**Durban**

M
T
S

D
R
A
K
E
N
S
B
E
R
G

• Umtata

Graaff-Reinet

Queenstown

Grahamstown

**East London**

Uitenhage

*INDIAN OCEAN*

**Port Elizabeth**

**Zulu dancing** is an impressive
sight. African dancing combines
rhythm, movement and music
to create a single art form.
Zulus are one of the main
groups of Bantu-speaking
people in South Africa.

**Lesotho** is a mountainous
country which depends mainly
on farming. About 80 per cent
of the people live in rural areas,
mainly in thatched houses
grouped in small villages.

**Rhinos** and other endangered
species are protected in Kruger
National Park in northeastern
South Africa, along the
Mozambique border. The park
was named after Paul Kruger,
leader of the Afrikaners (people
of Dutch descent), who fought
the British in the Boer Wars in
the late 19th century.

# PEOPLE AND BELIEFS

Africa is home to about 13 per cent of the world's population. Huge areas are thinly populated, others are overcrowded. Densely populated areas include the Nile valley and northwest coast, parts of West Africa, the lakelands of East Africa and southeastern Africa.

The Shona people of Zimbabwe traditionally used divining tablets like these to uncover secrets and tell the future.

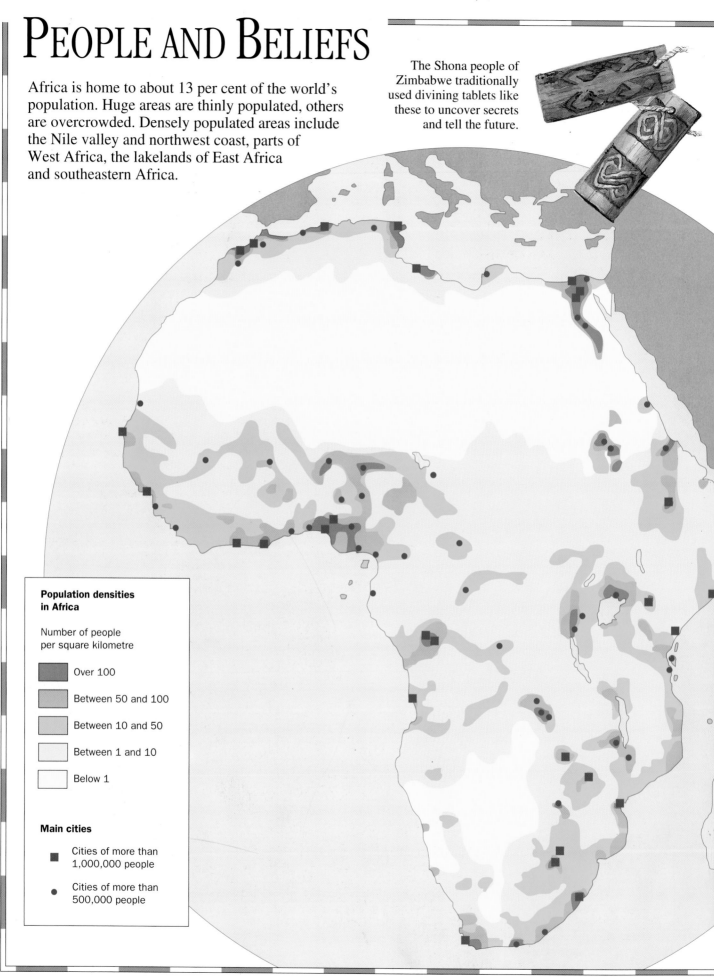

**Population densities in Africa**

Number of people per square kilometre

Over 100

Between 50 and 100

Between 10 and 50

Between 1 and 10

Below 1

**Main cities**

■ Cities of more than 1,000,000 people

● Cities of more than 500,000 people

## People and places

Africa's largest countries are Sudan, Algeria and the Democratic Republic of Congo. Sudan contains large, thinly populated deserts, swamps and humid rainforests, while many people are concentrated in the Nile valley. Nigeria, the 13th largest country, has the highest population in Africa. But the most crowded countries on the African mainland are Rwanda and Burundi. About one-third of Africa's people live in cities and towns. The largest city is Cairo.

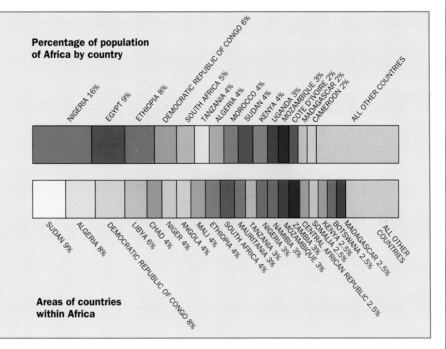

**Percentage of population of Africa by country**

NIGERIA 16% · EGYPT 9% · ETHIOPIA 8% · DEMOCRATIC REPUBLIC OF CONGO 6% · SOUTH AFRICA 5% · TANZANIA 4% · ALGERIA 4% · MOROCCO 4% · SUDAN 4% · KENYA 4% · UGANDA 3% · MOZAMBIQUE 3% · COTE D'IVOIRE 2% · MADAGASCAR 2% · CAMEROON 2% · ALL OTHER COUNTRIES

**Areas of countries within Africa**

SUDAN 9% · ALGERIA 8% · DEMOCRATIC REPUBLIC OF CONGO 8% · LIBYA 6% · CHAD 4% · NIGER 4% · ANGOLA 4% · MALI 4% · ETHIOPIA 4% · SOUTH AFRICA 4% · MAURITANIA 3% · TANZANIA 3% · NIGERIA 3% · NAMIBIA 3% · MOZAMBIQUE 3% · ZAMBIA 3% · CENTRAL AFRICAN REPUBLIC 2.5% · SOMALIA 2.5% · KENYA 2.5% · BOTSWANA 2.5% · MADAGASCAR 2.5% · ALL OTHER COUNTRIES

## Main religions

In the seventh century AD, Arabs spread from Arabia across North Africa, converting people to Islam. In the Middle Ages, Islam spread south of the Sahara, especially into West and East Africa. Today, about 41 per cent of Africa's people are Muslims. The Ethiopian Christian Church has existed since the fourth century AD. But Christianity did not reach most of Africa south of the Sahara until the 19th century. Today, nearly 49 per cent of the people of Africa are Christians. Most other Africans follow traditional religions. These religions vary, but all of them contain a belief in one supreme being.

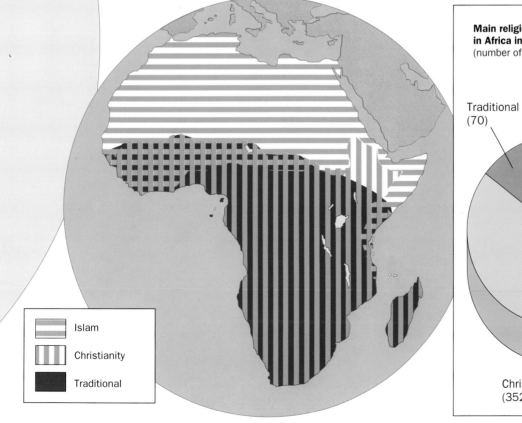

Islam
Christianity
Traditional

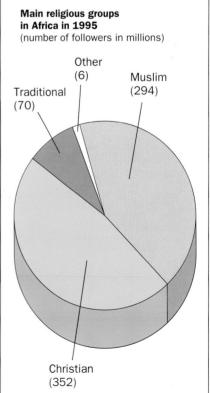

**Main religious groups in Africa in 1995**
(number of followers in millions)

Other (6)
Muslim (294)
Traditional (70)
Christian (352)

# CLIMATE AND VEGETATION

Rainforests grow in the tropical rainy climatic region around the equator. Savanna (grassland with scattered trees) occurs in places with tropical climates with wet and dry seasons. The savanna regions merge into dry grasslands and deserts. Mediterranean climates, with hot, dry summers and mild, rainy winters, occur in the far northwest and southwest.

Only about one-third of Africa's land is used for farming, though more than half the people are farmers.

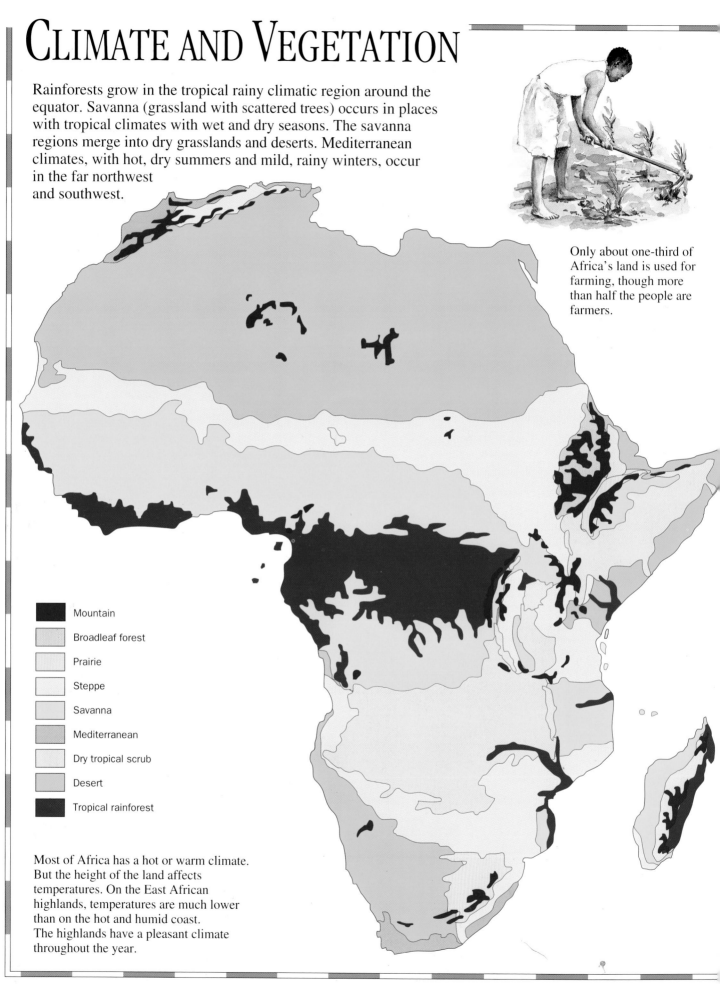

Mountain

Broadleaf forest

Prairie

Steppe

Savanna

Mediterranean

Dry tropical scrub

Desert

Tropical rainforest

Most of Africa has a hot or warm climate. But the height of the land affects temperatures. On the East African highlands, temperatures are much lower than on the hot and humid coast. The highlands have a pleasant climate throughout the year.

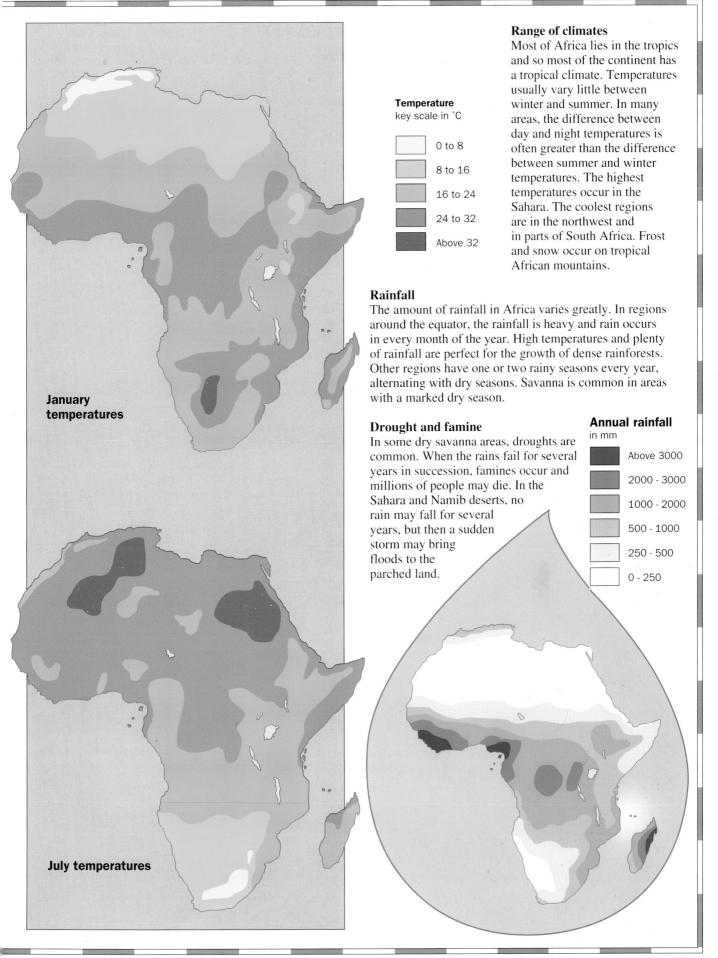

**Temperature**
key scale in °C

- 0 to 8
- 8 to 16
- 16 to 24
- 24 to 32
- Above 32

**January temperatures**

**July temperatures**

## Range of climates

Most of Africa lies in the tropics and so most of the continent has a tropical climate. Temperatures usually vary little between winter and summer. In many areas, the difference between day and night temperatures is often greater than the difference between summer and winter temperatures. The highest temperatures occur in the Sahara. The coolest regions are in the northwest and in parts of South Africa. Frost and snow occur on tropical African mountains.

## Rainfall

The amount of rainfall in Africa varies greatly. In regions around the equator, the rainfall is heavy and rain occurs in every month of the year. High temperatures and plenty of rainfall are perfect for the growth of dense rainforests. Other regions have one or two rainy seasons every year, alternating with dry seasons. Savanna is common in areas with a marked dry season.

## Drought and famine

In some dry savanna areas, droughts are common. When the rains fail for several years in succession, famines occur and millions of people may die. In the Sahara and Namib deserts, no rain may fall for several years, but then a sudden storm may bring floods to the parched land.

**Annual rainfall**
in mm

- Above 3000
- 2000 - 3000
- 1000 - 2000
- 500 - 1000
- 250 - 500
- 0 - 250

# ECOLOGY AND ENVIRONMENT

In the late 1990s, Africa's population was increasing by about 2.6 per cent per year – faster than any other continent. The rapid increase in population in the last 50 years has led to the destruction of forests and savanna, causing great damage to the land in many areas.

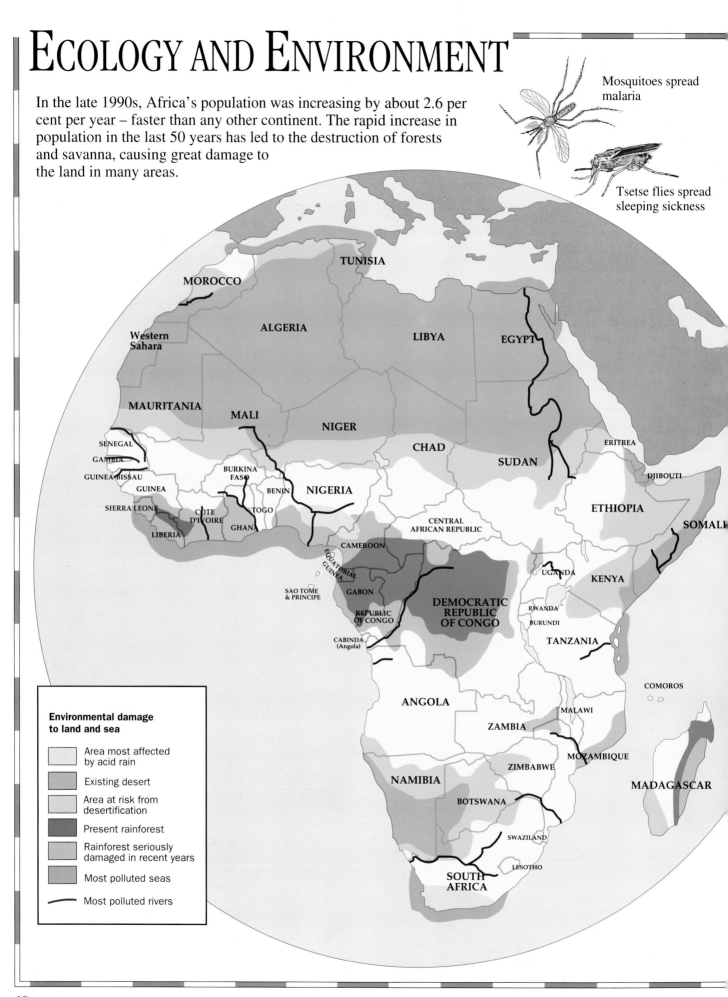

Mosquitoes spread malaria

Tsetse flies spread sleeping sickness

**Environmental damage to land and sea**

- Area most affected by acid rain
- Existing desert
- Area at risk from desertification
- Present rainforest
- Rainforest seriously damaged in recent years
- Most polluted seas
- Most polluted rivers

## Damaging the environment

The destruction of the natural plant life in any area exposes the soil. When forests are cut down to create farmland, the rain dissolves away plant nutrients in the soil. As a result, exposed soil in tropical rainy areas soon becomes infertile. Farmers then need to add expensive fertilizers to the soil to grow crops.

In dry areas, people graze cattle, sheep and goats. The larger the herds, the greater the destruction of the plants on which the animals feed. The herders also need fuel, so they cut down trees and shrubs. As the numbers of people and animals in dry grassland areas increase, so the rate of plant destruction increases. When the plants are removed, the dry soil is broken up into fine dust. This dust is often blown away by the wind or washed away by storms, leaving bare rock on which nothing can grow. This is called soil erosion.

## Natural hazards

Unreliable rainfall and occasional long droughts are major natural hazards in Africa. Droughts lasting several years have occurred in the Sahel. Already scanty vegetation, unable to support an increasing population of people and livestock, has been stripped to bare earth and rock. This process, called desertification, turns once fertile land into desert. The people must migrate or starve. Other hazards include diseases, such as malaria, sleeping sickness and AIDS. Diseases disable and kill millions of cattle and people.

**Natural hazards and diseases**

- Earthquake zones
- AIDS widespread
- Malaria widespread
- Sleeping sickness widespread
- Areas recently affected by famine

## Endangered species

Only 50 years ago, the forests and grasslands of Africa supported enormous numbers of wild animals. But the rapid increase in Africa's population has led to widespread destruction of forests and savanna regions once occupied only by animals. Many countries have set up national parks to conserve wildlife. These parks are tourist attractions.

Many animals have been killed for food or for profit. Poachers slaughter elephants for their tusks and all kinds of animals die when people fight wars where they live. For example, in the eastern Democratic Republic of Congo, the endangered mountain gorillas were threatened by warfare in the 1990s.

Black rhino

**Some endangered species of Africa**

**Birds**
Hermit ibis
Congo peacock
Mauritius kestrel
White-necked picathartes

**Mammals**
African hunting dog
Aye-aye
Black rhino
Grevy's zebra
Mountain gorilla

**Marine mammals**
Leatherback turtle

**Plants**
Afrormosia tree
Madagascar periwinkle
Mulanje cedar
Giant protea

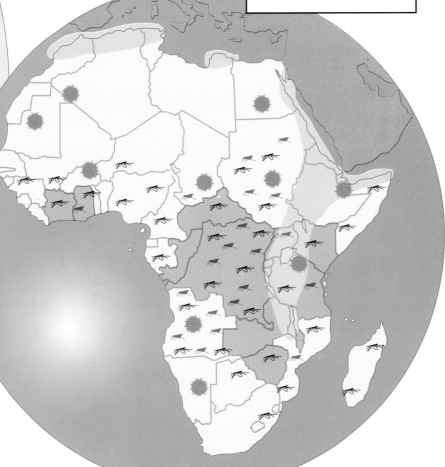

# ECONOMY

Africa has many natural resources, including oil and natural gas, and huge deposits of valuable metals and precious stones. Most of the fuels and minerals are exported, however, because Africa lacks the industries to process them. About 60 per cent of Africa's people live by farming. Many farmers are poor, producing little more than they need to support their families.

The huge rivers of Africa are capable of producing enormous amounts of electric power.

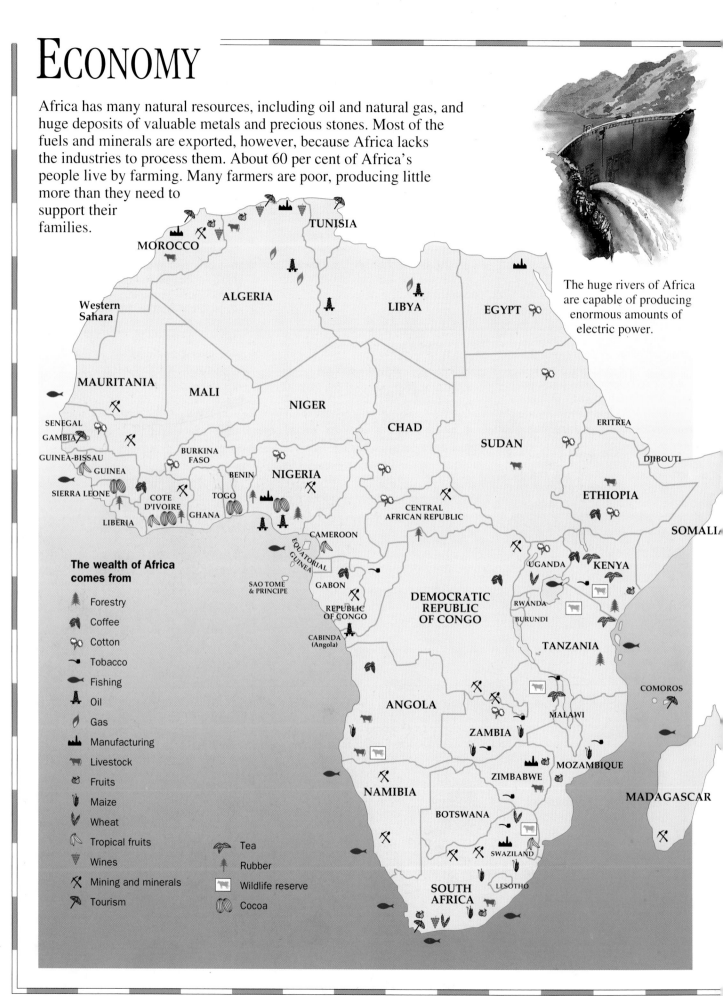

**The wealth of Africa comes from**

- Forestry
- Coffee
- Cotton
- Tobacco
- Fishing
- Oil
- Gas
- Manufacturing
- Livestock
- Fruits
- Maize
- Wheat
- Tropical fruits
- Wines
- Mining and minerals
- Tourism
- Tea
- Rubber
- Wildlife reserve
- Cocoa

**Country labels:**
MOROCCO, TUNISIA, ALGERIA, LIBYA, EGYPT, Western Sahara, MAURITANIA, MALI, NIGER, CHAD, SUDAN, ERITREA, DJIBOUTI, SENEGAL, GAMBIA, GUINEA-BISSAU, GUINEA, BURKINA FASO, BENIN, NIGERIA, CENTRAL AFRICAN REPUBLIC, ETHIOPIA, SOMALIA, SIERRA LEONE, COTE D'IVOIRE, TOGO, GHANA, LIBERIA, CAMEROON, EQUATORIAL GUINEA, SAO TOME & PRINCIPE, GABON, REPUBLIC OF CONGO, DEMOCRATIC REPUBLIC OF CONGO, UGANDA, KENYA, RWANDA, BURUNDI, CABINDA (Angola), TANZANIA, COMOROS, ANGOLA, MALAWI, ZAMBIA, MOZAMBIQUE, ZIMBABWE, NAMIBIA, BOTSWANA, SWAZILAND, MADAGASCAR, SOUTH AFRICA, LESOTHO

## Gross national product

In order to compare the economies of countries, experts work out the gross national product (GNP) of the countries in US dollars. The GNP is the total value of all the goods and services produced in a country in a year. The pie chart, right, shows that South Africa's GNP is the highest in Africa. It is more than twice as large as Egypt's, the country with the second highest GNP. South Africa and Egypt have more industries than any other African country.

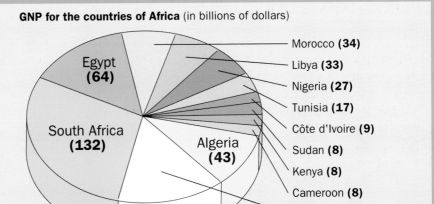

**GNP for the countries of Africa** (in billions of dollars)

Egypt (64)
South Africa (132)
Algeria (43)
Morocco (34)
Libya (33)
Nigeria (27)
Tunisia (17)
Côte d'Ivoire (9)
Sudan (8)
Kenya (8)
Cameroon (8)
All other African countries (80)

## Sources of energy

Although Africa mostly lacks coal, several countries produce oil and natural gas. Major exporters include Nigeria, Libya and Algeria. Egypt is another oil producer, but it uses most of its oil. Algeria, Africa's leading producer of natural gas, is one of the world's top ten producers. South Africa is Africa's only major producer of coal.

Hydroelectricity (water power) is important in countries with long rivers. For example, a major hydroelectric plant is located at the High Dam on the River Nile at Aswan, Egypt. The Democratic Republic of Congo, Ghana and Mozambique also have large hydroelectric power projects, while Zambia and Zimbabwe share the Kariba Gorge hydroelectric complex on the Zambezi River.

## Per capita GNPs

Per capita means per head or per person. Per capita GNPs are worked out by dividing the GNP by the population. South Africa's per capita GNP is US $3,520, much lower than the United States's per capita GNP of $28,020. But many African countries are poor, with extremely low per capita GNPs. For example, the per capita GNP of Mozambique is only $80.

**Sources of energy found in Africa**

- Oil
- Gas
- Hydroelectricity
- Coal
- Uranium

# POLITICS AND HISTORY

Africa contains 53 independent countries. Morocco in North Africa and Lesotho and Swaziland in southern Africa are monarchies. Morocco occupies Western Sahara, but some local people believe that it should be a separate, independent country. Most African countries are republics though many are not fully democratic.

Since achieving independence, the progress of many countries has been slowed by instability. Civil wars and military takeovers have occurred in many countries, with military leaders replacing civilian governments.

### Great events

Fossil evidence suggests that the evolution of the human species may have taken place in Africa.

Around 3100 BC, northeastern Africa was the site of a great early civilization, Ancient Egypt. In the Middle Ages, several major kingdoms, such as Ancient Ghana and Mali, flourished in West Africa. We owe our knowledge of these kingdoms to the Arabs, who traded with them.

European influence south of the Sahara began in the 15th century. At first, Europeans seldom went inland. Instead, they traded for slaves, gold and other valuable goods on the coast. In the late 19th century, most of Africa came under European rule. But from the 1950s, the countries of Africa gradually won their independence. In 1994, South Africa held its first election with all of its citizens being able to vote. Nelson Mandela was elected president.

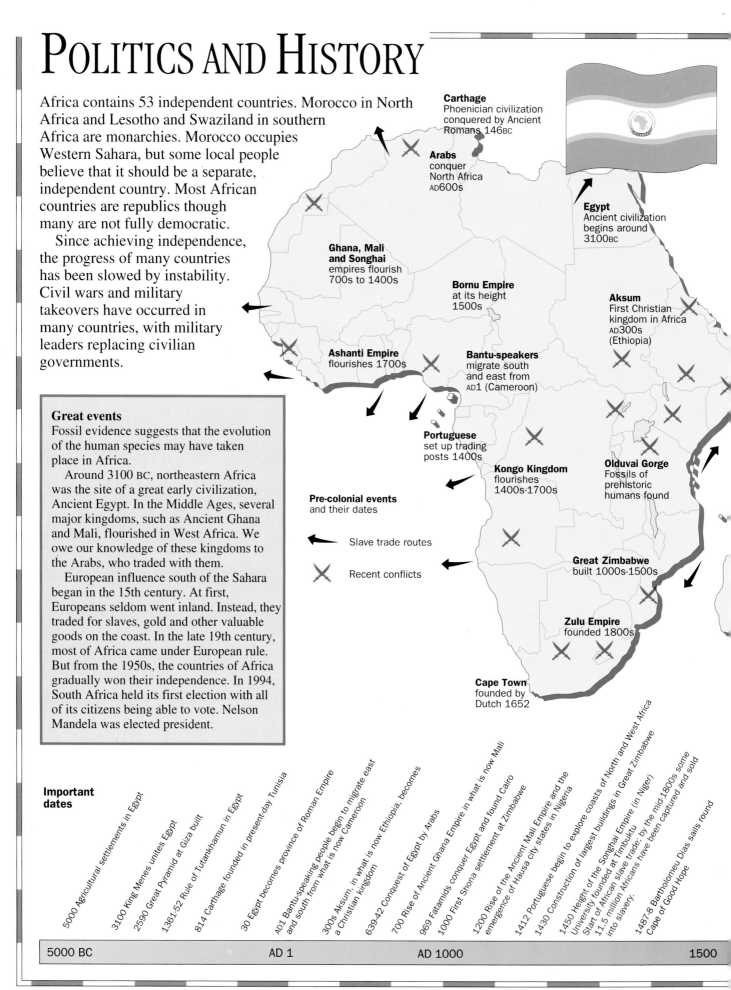

**Carthage**
Phoenician civilization conquered by Ancient Romans 146BC

**Arabs** conquer North Africa AD600s

**Egypt**
Ancient civilization begins around 3100BC

**Ghana, Mali and Songhai** empires flourish 700s to 1400s

**Bornu Empire** at its height 1500s

**Aksum**
First Christian kingdom in Africa AD300s (Ethiopia)

**Ashanti Empire** flourishes 1700s

**Bantu-speakers** migrate south and east from AD1 (Cameroon)

**Portuguese** set up trading posts 1400s

**Kongo Kingdom** flourishes 1400s-1700s

**Olduvai Gorge**
Fossils of prehistoric humans found

**Pre-colonial events** and their dates

→ Slave trade routes

✗ Recent conflicts

**Great Zimbabwe** built 1000s-1500s

**Zulu Empire** founded 1800s

**Cape Town** founded by Dutch 1652

**Important dates**

5000 Agricultural settlements in Egypt

3100 King Menes unites Egypt

2590 Great Pyramid at Giza built

1361-52 Rule of Tutankhamun in Egypt

814 Carthage founded in present-day Tunisia

30 Egypt becomes province of Roman Empire

AD1 Bantu-speaking people begin to migrate east and south from what is now Cameroon

300s Aksum, in what is now Ethiopia, becomes a Christian kingdom

639-42 Conquest of Egypt by Arabs

700 Rise of Ancient Ghana Empire in what is now Mali

969 Fatamids conquer Egypt and found Cairo

1000 First Shona settlement at Zimbabwe

1200 Rise of the Ancient Mali Empire and the emergence of Hausa city states in Nigeria

1412 Portuguese begin to explore coasts of North and West Africa

1430 Construction of largest buildings in Great Zimbabwe

1450 Height of the Songhai Empire (in Niger) University founded at Timbuktu Start of African slave trade; by the mid-1800s some 11.5 million Africans have been captured and sold into slavery.

1487-8 Bartholomeu Dias sails round Cape of Good Hope

| 5000 BC | AD 1 | AD 1000 | 1500 |

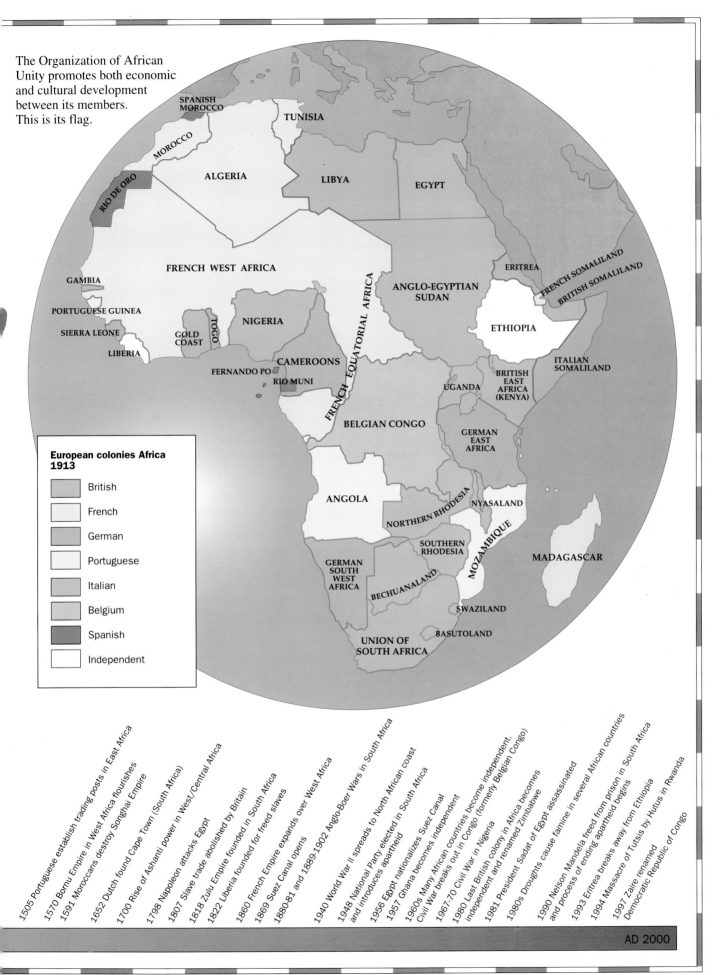

The Organization of African Unity promotes both economic and cultural development between its members. This is its flag.

**European colonies Africa 1913**

- British
- French
- German
- Portuguese
- Italian
- Belgium
- Spanish
- Independent

SPANISH MOROCCO
TUNISIA
MOROCCO
ALGERIA
LIBYA
EGYPT
RIO DE ORO
FRENCH WEST AFRICA
ERITREA
FRENCH SOMALILAND
BRITISH SOMALILAND
ANGLO-EGYPTIAN SUDAN
GAMBIA
PORTUGUESE GUINEA
NIGERIA
ETHIOPIA
SIERRA LEONE
GOLD COAST
TOGO
LIBERIA
CAMEROONS
FERNANDO PO
RIO MUNI
ITALIAN SOMALILAND
FRENCH EQUATORIAL AFRICA
UGANDA
BRITISH EAST AFRICA (KENYA)
BELGIAN CONGO
GERMAN EAST AFRICA
ANGOLA
NYASALAND
NORTHERN RHODESIA
MOZAMBIQUE
MADAGASCAR
GERMAN SOUTH WEST AFRICA
SOUTHERN RHODESIA
BECHUANALAND
SWAZILAND
BASUTOLAND
UNION OF SOUTH AFRICA

1505 Portuguese establish trading posts in East Africa
1570 Bornu Empire in West Africa flourishes
1591 Moroccans destroy Songhai Empire
1652 Dutch found Cape Town (South Africa)
1700 Rise of Ashanti power in West/Central Africa
1798 Napoleon attacks Egypt
1807 Slave trade abolished by Britain
1818 Zulu Empire founded in South Africa
1822 Liberia founded for freed slaves
1860 French Empire expands over West Africa
1869 Suez Canal opens
1880-81 and 1889-1902 Anglo-Boer Wars in South Africa
1940 World War II spreads to North African coast
1948 National Party elected in South Africa and introduces apartheid
1956 Egypt nationalizes Suez Canal
1957 Ghana becomes independent
1960s Many African countries become independent
1967-70 Civil War in Nigeria
1980 Last British colony in Africa becomes independent and renamed Zimbabwe
Civil War breaks out in Congo (formerly Belgian Congo)
1981 President Sadat of Egypt assassinated
1980s Droughts cause famine in several African countries
1990 Nelson Mandela freed from prison in South Africa and process of ending apartheid begins
1993 Eritrea breaks away from Ethiopia
1994 Massacre of Tutsis by Hutus in Rwanda
1997 Zaire renamed Democratic Republic of Congo

AD 2000

45

# INDEX

Numbers in **bold** are map references
Numbers in *italics* are picture references

**Picture credits**
**Photographs:** AS Publishing 9
The Hutchison Library 6, 11, 12, 15, 18, 20, 25, 29, 30, 33
Travel Photo International 27, 34